BOYNE AND BEYOND:
essays in appreciation of George Eogan

Edited by Peigín Doyle

Wordwell

BOYNE AND BEYOND:
essays in appreciation of George Eogan

First published 2024
by Wordwell Ltd,
in association with National Monuments Service

Wordwell Ltd.,
Unit 9, 78 Furze Road,
Sandyford Industrial Estate,
Dublin 18, Eircode D18 C6V6
T: + 353-1-2933568
www.wordwellbooks.com
ISBN 978-1-913934-95-8

Acknowledgements: The publisher would like to acknowledge the collaboration offered by the authors of the separate papers to Peigín Doyle in producing this work, which reflects their individual contributions to the Boyne and Beyond conference held at Dublin Castle on 02 October 2022 and the financial contribution of the Department of Housing, Local Government and Heritage toward the book's production costs.

Contributors: Joanna Brück, Kerri Cleary, Stuart Needham, Clíodhna Ní Lionáin, Elizabeth Shee Twohig, Alison Sheridan and Neil Wilkin
Consulting editor: Sharon Greene
Commissioning editor: Una MacConville
Editor: Peigín Doyle
Production editor: Nick Maxwell
Design: Ger Garland
Layout: © Wordwell Ltd.
Printer: W & G Bairds, Antrim

All rights reserved. No part of this publication may be reprinted or reproduced or utilised in any form by electronic, mechanical or other means, now known or hereafter invented, including photocopying and recording, or otherwise without either the prior written consent of the publisher or a licence permitting restricted copying in Ireland issued by the Irish Copyright Licensing Agency Ltd, The Writers' Centre, 19 Parnell Square, Dublin 1.

The right of the author and collaborators to be identified as the authors of this work has been asserted in accordance with the Copyright and Related Rights Act, 2000.

CONTENTS

Foreword	5
Introduction: James Eogan	8
Chapter 1: What Lies Beneath? Uncovering the story of Knowth through time Kerri Cleary	10
Chapter 2: Exploring The Life Cycle of a Forgotten Monument: The Dowth Hall Passage Tomb Excavation Clíodhna Ní Lionáin	36
Chapter 3: Bronze Age Relations: Genetics, Kinship and Gender in Later Prehistory Joanna Brück	58
Chapter 4: From Barrowscape to Fieldscape: The first fields in the Rother Region of the Western Weald Stuart Needham	74
Chapter 5: Megalithic Art in the Boyne Valley and beyond Elizabeth Shee Twohig	88
Chapter 6: Ireland in the Wider Prehistoric World, 4300 – 1750 BC Alison Sheridan	110
Chapter 7: Lives that Bind: Three Stories from the World of Stonehenge Neil Wilkin	140
Image Credits	158
Biographies	164

Newgrange, 3300 BC — older than Giza Pyramids (2600 BC) and Stonehenge (2500 BC).

FOREWORD

The UNESCO World Heritage property of Brú na Bóinne is home to some of Ireland's most remarkable archaeological heritage, including Ireland's finest passage tomb cemeteries and the great mounds of Knowth, Dowth and Newgrange.

Our National Monuments Service 2022 Conference, organized with *Archaeology Ireland* and in partnership with the Office of Public Works, explored that remarkable heritage of the Boyne Valley in the context of the wider prehistoric world. We framed this as a tribute to Professor George Eogan, whose lifetime of work, including at Knowth, augmented our knowledge of prehistoric Ireland immensely, providing significant contributions to our understanding of the monuments and their landscape through the millennia. It was also a testimony to the work of the many other experts who have devoted their time to researching this heritage.

We explored the monuments within their landscape, including through a prism of connections with Scotland, Wales and England. The landscape of Brú na Bóinne, now cared for by communities and the State, by farmers and landowners, is a very special one, which continues to reveal yet more archaeological wonders, as we heard about at Dowth Hall.

Our conference theme also illustrated our commitment to ensuring that these monuments and their landscape are protected and enjoyed by many for generations to come.

I would like to thank *Archaeology Ireland* for their expertise in bringing the conference together with our National Monuments Service. We are grateful for this partnership and commend *Archaeology Ireland* and all the speakers for the admirable achievement of bringing these conference proceedings to publication in such a short time. We are also grateful to the OPW for our important heritage partnership and for the use of Dublin Castle as our official conference venue. My final thanks are to all who attended our conference for making it such a wonderful event and for joining us in celebrating our wonderful archaeological heritage, which enriches our lives immeasurably.

Malcolm Noonan TD
Minister of State for Heritage and Electoral Reform

Jamb stone at the right side of the rear recess in the eastern chamber of the large mound at Knowth.

BROLLACH

Tá cuid den oidhreacht seandálaíochta is suntasaí in Éirinn, lena n-áirítear na reiligí tuama pasáiste is fearr in Éirinn agus tuamaí móra Chnóbha, Dhubhadh agus Shí an Bhrú lonnaithe i láithreán oidhreachta domhanda EOECNA Bhrú na Bóinne.

Rinne Comhdháil Sheirbhís na Séadchomharthaí Náisiúnta 2022, a eagraíodh le *Seandálaíocht Éireann* agus i gcomhpháirtíocht le hOifig na nOibreacha Poiblí, iniúchadh ar oidhreacht shuntasach Ghleann na Bóinne i gcomhthéacs an domhain réamhstairiúil i gcoitinne. Ómós don Ollamh George Eogan a bhí san imeacht. Duine ab ea an tOllamh ar chuir a shaol oibre, lena n-áirítear ag Cnóbha, go mór lenár n-eolas ar Éirinn réamhstairiúil, rud a chur go mór lenár dtuiscint ar na séadchomharthaí agus ar a dtírdhreach le linn na mílte bliain. Ba léiriú a bhí ann freisin ar obair an iliomad saineolaithe eile a chaith a gcuid ama ag déanamh taighde ar an oidhreacht seo.

Rinneamar iniúchadh ar na séadchomharthaí laistigh dá dtírdhreach, lena n-áirítear trí phriosma de naisc le hAlbain, leis an mBreatain Bheag agus le Sasana. Tá tírdhreach Bhrú na Bóinne, atá anois faoi chúram an phobail agus an Stáit, chomh maith le feirmeoirí agus úinéirí talún, ina thírdhreach an-speisialta a leanann de bheith ag nochtadh tuilleadh iontais seandálaíochta fós, mar a chualamar ag Halla Dhubhadh.

Léirigh téama ár gcomhdhála freisin ár dtiomantas chun a chinntiú go ndéantar na séadchomharthaí seo agus a dtírdhreach a chosaint agus go mbaineann na glúnta atá le teacht taitneamh astu.

Ba mhaith liom buíochas a ghabháil le *Seandálaíocht Éireann* as a gcuid saineolais agus an chomhdháil á tabhairt le chéile i gcomhpháirt le Seirbhís na Séadchomharthaí Náisiúnta. Táimid buíoch as an gcomhpháirtíocht seo agus molaimid *Seandálaíocht Éireann* agus na cainteoirí go léir as an éacht iontach a bhain le himeachtaí na comhdhála seo a thabhairt chun foilsithe in achar gearr. Gabhaimid buíochas freisin le hOifig na nOibreacha Poiblí as ár gcomhpháirtíocht oidhreachta thábhachtach agus as cead a thabhairt dúinn Caisleán Bhaile Átha Cliath a úsáid mar ár n-ionad oifigiúil comhdhála. Mar fhocal scoir, ba mhaith liom buíochas a ghabháil le gach duine a d'fhreastail ar ár gcomhdháil as imeacht iontach a dhéanamh de agus as a bheith linn chun ár n-oidhreacht iontach seandálaíochta a cheiliúradh, oidhreacht a chuireann lenár saolta go mór.

Malcolm Noonan TD
Aire Stáit Oidhreachta agus Athchóirithe Toghcháin

Above: **George Eogan excavating at Fourknocks in July 1952.**

INTRODUCTION

The National Monuments Service generously dedicated the 2022 annual archaeology conference on the theme of *Boyne and Beyond: Examining the Boyne Valley monuments in the context of the wider prehistoric world* to the memory of my dad, George Eogan. I hope that, as you read the contributions brought together in this book and reflect on his life's work, you also think of all those who enabled the boy, raised in modest circumstances in Nobber, County Meath, to develop his interest in archaeology, which has left us a rich legacy of scholarship.

Dad was fortunate to have had a number of significant mentors in his life. As a schoolboy in Nobber, his teacher, Michael Falvey, brought him and his classmates on an outing to Newgrange. It was Michael Falvey that first fired Dad's interest and curiosity in the subject that would become his life's passion.

Having completed his secondary education, he worked in various jobs and pursued his interest in archaeology through membership of the Royal Society of Antiquaries of Ireland. This gave him the confidence, as an 18-year-old, to write to the National Museum of Ireland to enquire about the possibility of employment on any excavations they were conducting in the Meath area. The Museum offered him work with Paddy Hartnett, the University College Cork-trained archaeologist. Hartnett saw something in this young man, unqualified but enthusiastic, and in time he became Dad's great mentor. Not only did he employ him on excavations, most notably at Fourknocks passage tomb, County Meath, he also introduced him to the world of archaeology and the network of Irish and international archaeologists.

When Paddy was appointed the first Archaeological Officer of Bord Fáilte, as Fáilte Ireland, the Irish Tourist Board, was then called, he required an assistant and fortunately for Dad his application was successful. The job gave him the opportunity to visit historic sites around the country and, crucially, it provided the income that enabled him to enrol in the night degree course in archaeology in University College Dublin. I think it is fair to say that these formative experiences influenced the way that he encouraged generations of students and members of the public that he interacted with over his long career.

In the 1950s and 1960s, he took the opportunity to travel, attending conferences, studying in the Institute of Archaeology, Oxford, visiting notable sites and museums and participating in excavations in Britain, on the Continent and in the Levant. This inspired him to seek to understand how the archaeology of this island on the periphery of Europe related to these better-studied regions. This experience also showed him the value of collaboration with individuals and institutions, in Ireland and abroad, and the value of interdisciplinary research. He would have been delighted with the emphasis on the examination of prehistoric Ireland's international connections by the speakers at the *Boyne and Beyond* conference.

It hardly needs to be said that Dad was a hard worker; his published output speaks for itself. However, I cannot let the opportunity pass without observing that Dad loved to dig. The physical act of digging gave him pleasure whether on site or in the garden. Long before manual handling training was a requirement for work on excavations, he used to instruct students and workmen at Knowth on the proper way to dig with a spade and to shovel spoil, bending your knees and minding your back. It was the shared experiences of labouring together that made the excavations at Knowth such a formative experience for so many, myself included. Of course, it was not just the work of excavation, peeling back the layers of time and revealing the sequence of development of the site and the people who had lived and were buried there but the social aspect of excavation that was so enjoyable. Field trips to sites in the locality and sometimes further afield, nights in Lev Mitchell's pub in Rossin, the collective meals in Townley Hall that my mother provided for the hungry hordes after a day's labouring, the annual Knowth Party when a keg of Guinness was ceremoniously escorted onto the site by the local piper Davy McGuinness all added to the memories.

Notwithstanding all the fun, Dad understood the importance of ensuring that the results of the excavations at Knowth and other sites, and his research on Bronze Age material culture – swords, hoards, axes and gold – were shared with the public who ultimately had funded the research. One of Dad's first jobs when assisting Paddy Hartnett involved the installation by Bord Fáilte of electric light in Newgrange passage tomb. It is nice to think of this as a metaphorical beginning to an archaeological career that over seven decades shed significant new light on the Bronze Age in Ireland and the archaeology of Brú na Bóinne. Dad's research expanded our knowledge of and appreciation for Ireland's archaeological heritage. He was energized by knowing that his research stimulated other scholars who, using new investigative techniques and methodological approaches, continue this work.

On behalf of the Eogan family I would like to acknowledge Minister of State with responsibility for Heritage and Electoral Reform Malcolm Noonan, TD, Michael MacDonagh, Chief Archaeologist, and the National Monuments Service Ireland for dedicating the *Boyne and Beyond* conference to Dad; Sharon Greene, Una MacConville, Nick Maxwell and the *Archaeology Ireland* team for their organization; and all the speakers who delivered such stimulating talks on the day and then prepared them for publication in this book.

James Eogan

Chapter 1:

The multidisciplinary and collaborative nature of the project was something that George Eogan was very cognizant of from the beginning.

DR KERRI CLEARY

What Lies Beneath? Uncovering the Story of Knowth Through Time

Dr Kerri Cleary worked alongside Professor George Eogan for many years. As co-ordinator of the Knowth Publication Project 2007–2010, she collaborated with him in preparing for publication by the Royal Irish Academy the sixth volume of the *Excavations at Knowth* series, which focused on the largest passage tomb. Here she tells the story of Knowth as a complex, multi-period site, highlighting certain aspects, and the legacy of the discoveries for archaeology and wider society.

The three so-called 'mega-mounds' of Knowth, Dowth and Newgrange sit on the natural shale ridges that run through the landscape along the bend of the Boyne River, or Brú na Bóinne, in County Meath. The course of the river itself has probably changed very little since the Neolithic, although it may have been slightly wider and shallower at that time.

Left: The excavations in the early 1970s, looking north-east, with the cuttings into the large mound visible centre.

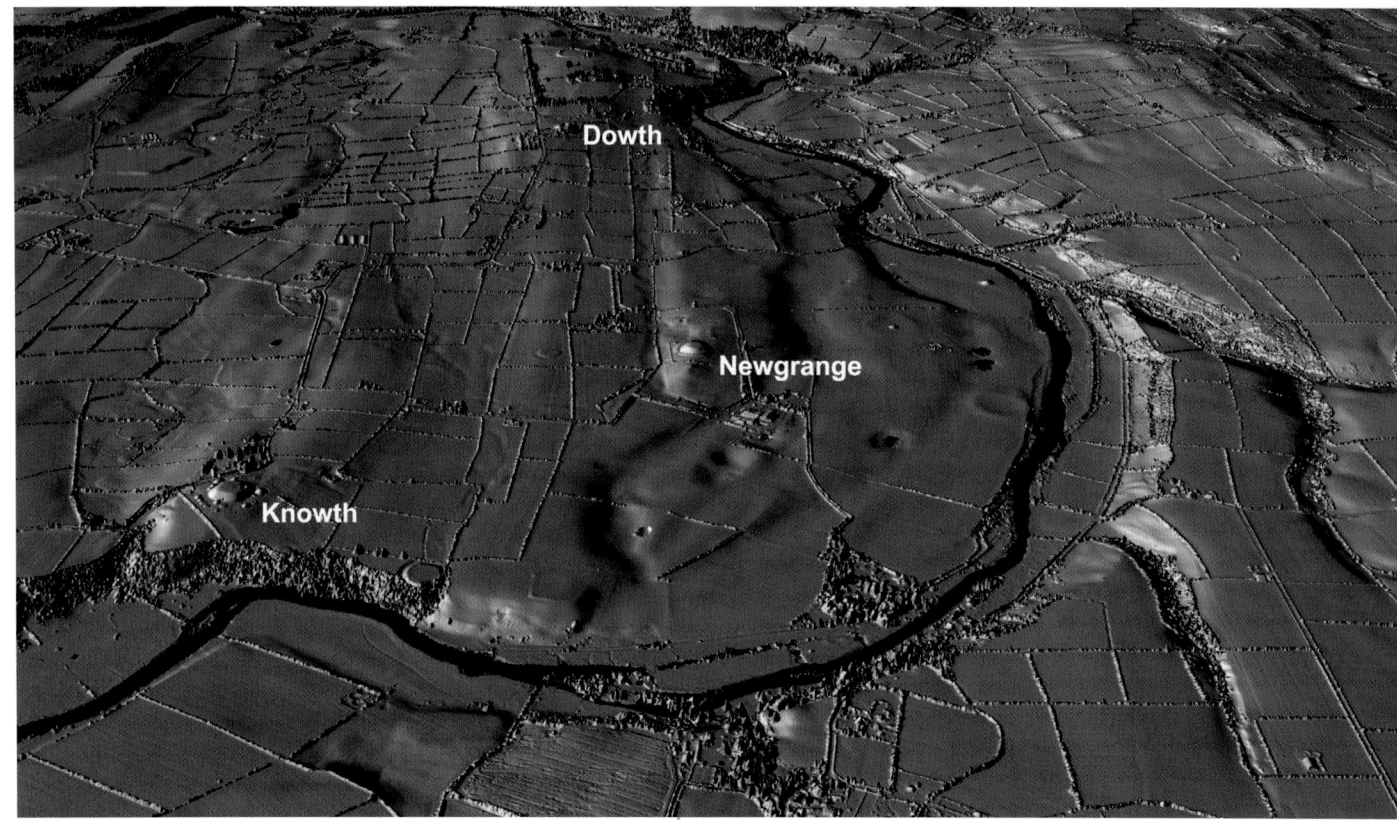

By the time Professor Eogan began excavations at Knowth, on 18 June 1962, very little had changed since the 1830s, when John O'Donovan of the Ordnance Survey of Ireland had commented on the failure of efforts to discover a passage into the large mound (Herity 1967). Similar references to the site followed throughout the nineteenth and early twentieth centuries but still very little was known about what lay beneath the mound. This contrasted quite significantly with Newgrange, where the passage into the chamber had been discovered as early as 1699.

When excavations began, the largest passage tomb at Knowth was still very much a grass-covered mound approximately 90 metres in diameter and 10 metres in height. The tops of a few of the kerbstones were visible, primarily on the north-western perimeter, and there was a channel leading up to the summit where

Above: **A LiDAR-generated image of Brú na Bóinne with the main passage tomb sites marked.**

Opposite page: **Knowth as it appeared in 1963, a year after excavations started, looking to the south-west.**
Reproduced with permission of the Cambridge Collection of Aerial Photography (©) Copyright reserved.

there was also a substantial depression. This depression is believed to have been caused by people quarrying through the mound in advance of building roads and houses in the locality since at least the 1830s, probably earlier.

The area around the mound was largely grass-covered flatland, except where there were traces of a smaller tomb, which is what we know now as Tomb 14. This was initially excavated by R.A.S. Macalister over a period of three weeks in the summer of 1941.

Macalister, who was the first professor of Celtic Archaeology in University College Dublin (UCD), had also tried to find an entrance into the large mound but had not succeeded. Aside from Tomb 14, his investigations did uncover the outer faces of 58 of the kerbstones around the large mound. This not only revealed some of the megalithic art that can be seen today but also alerted the team to the importance of the site.

MODERN EXCAVATIONS

So, when George Eogan started his work in 1962, he decided to focus on some stones to the west of Tomb 14, on what is known now as Tomb 12. From there, the excavations largely continued seasonally for the next 38 years. From early in the investigations, it became very clear that Knowth was a complex, multi-period site with layers of occupation preserved directly underneath the grass and sod.

It is also important to remember that much of the excavation work was undertaken to enable a parallel programme of conservation and restoration. So, while the flat areas surrounding the largest passage tomb mound have been extensively archaeologically investigated, much of the footprint of the large mound itself actually remains unexcavated to this day. Indeed, only a very small number of cuttings extended far enough into the mound to uncover the old ground surface that is preserved beneath it.

In 1967, 130 years after O'Donovan had pointed out the failure to discover the passageway into the large mound, the mystery was solved when what was thought to be the only entrance was located. In the words of George Eogan: '. . . we thought that was the only structure that existed in the big mound because, as far as we could know, there was only one such structure at Newgrange. And we therefore thought that we had discovered

Opposite page: **Aerial view of Knowth as it is today, 60 years after excavations started.**

Above: **Artist's impression of settlement at Knowth in the Early Neolithic.**

EARLY ACTIVITY

A series of artist's impressions completed by Steve Doogan in 2018 for the Knowth exhibition illustrate how the site was used and reused over this time. One such image gives an impression of what the landscape may have looked like when the early farmers first settled here around 3700 BC, clearing some woodland and building a series of houses on the shale ridge (p15). These first people left a very definite trace at the site. They had round-bottom Carinated Bowl pottery, they used worked flint and quartz tools, and they raised wheat, barley, cattle and pigs. Evidence for their occupation on the shale ridge was largely preserved to the north and the east of the site.

Slightly later, two rectangular structures called Houses A and B were built to the west. These are also associated with Carinated Bowls, although with more expanded rims and developed shoulders, as well as more accomplished stone tools that included the use of chert. The remains of two arcs of palisade trenches may also date broadly to this period. To the west of these there were areas of flint knapping, stone surfaces and pits. The dating of these structures and their relationship to one another remains somewhat elusive but an associated stone axehead and two stone beads, as well as some Carinated Bowl pottery and lithics, certainly point to a Neolithic date. The fact that the eastern palisade was erected after House B had fallen out of use underlines that this was a site that was being occupied over quite a long period. Some time later, the site appears to have been abandoned and a layer of sod developed over these structures, suggesting that the site probably returned

the tomb at Knowth. But then the astonishing thing was, the following year, in 1968, we continued on the excavations and discovered even a larger and greater site on the opposite side of the large mound. So, within two seasons, we discovered two vast tombs'.

An aerial image of what Knowth looks like today, after those excavation and conservation works, is largely a reconstruction of the passage tomb cemetery. This in itself is just a snapshot of one stage, of one phase, of many phases of building, occupation and demolition that George Eogan's investigations identified. Occupation began in at least the Early Neolithic, around 3700 BC, and continued on and off over the next roughly 5,500 years.

Above: **Carinated Bowl pottery similar to this reconstructed vessel was found at Knowth.**

Opposite page: **Evidence for earlier settlement, discovered around and beneath the passage tombs.**

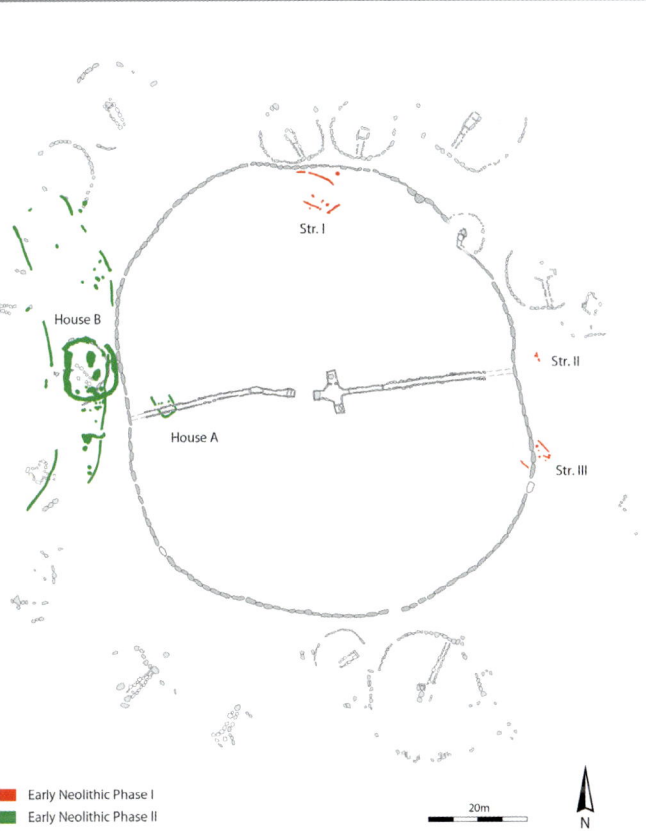
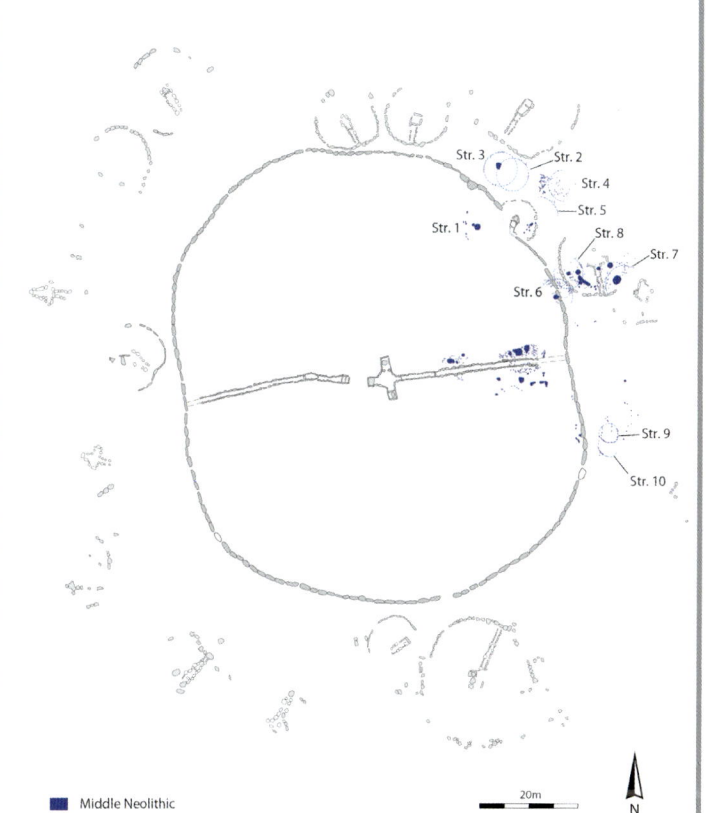

again to land that was suitable for mixed farming.

TOMB BUILDING

A few hundred years later, around 3200 BC but probably slightly earlier, this shale ridge became the focus of an intense period of tomb building. Another artist's impression (pg 18) gives a sense of the site under construction and demonstrates how the large mound was built in at least two stages. This created the mega-mound that we know today and that is comparable to those at Dowth and Newgrange.

To build this cemetery also took considerable resources. This included stripping the ground of sods that were subsequently built back into the tomb mounds. Such a practice would also have left the area devoid of farmable land at this stage.

Another important discovery that came to light was the evidence for contemporary circular, post-built structures, hearths and pits. These were preserved underneath the passage tombs and were concentrated on the northeast and east sides of the site. This suggested

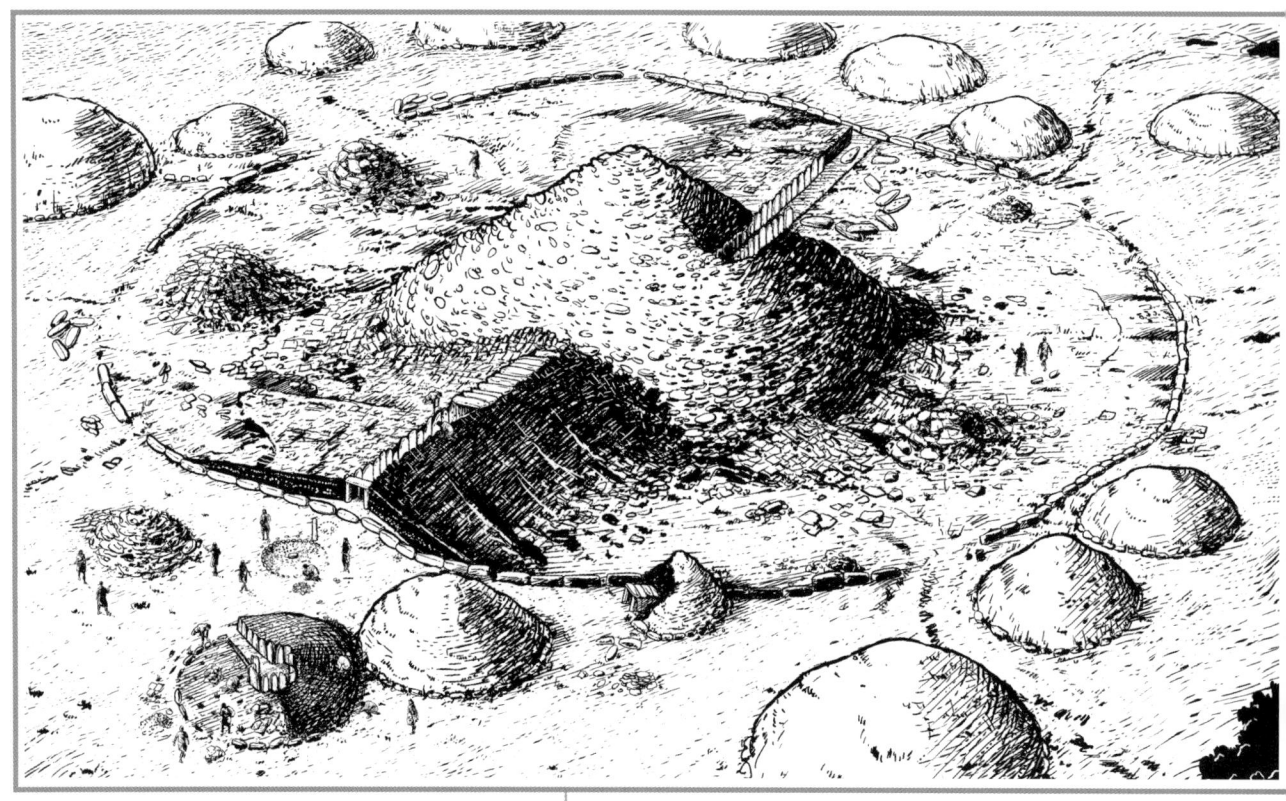

that there was occupation on the ridge around the time that the tombs were being constructed. It is tempting to see these features as a shadow of the people who built the monuments and probably also used them. These people also had round-bottomed pots that we call Carrowkeel Ware or Broad-rimmed Ware, as well as worked chert and flint, and they consumed cattle, pig and wheat. Some structures overlapped, suggesting that they may have had short lifespans or might even have been moved around the site as required, perhaps, for example, if work on the tombs was seasonal. Some buttercup and insect remains that were found in the sod layers of the largest tomb have suggested a time of late spring to late summer for when these sods were being harvested and used to build up the mounds (Davis 2017).

Above: **Artist's impression of the building of the large mound and some of the smaller tombs.**

Opposite page: **The footprint of the large tomb in its first and second stages, with the V-shaped entrances visible in the first phase (in green).**

Regarding the cemetery itself, although the exact sequence of tomb building at Knowth still remains a little bit speculative, the excavations did demonstrate that the large tomb was constructed in at least two stages. The first stage is referred to now as Tomb 1B and the second as Tomb 1C. It was also clear that some of the smaller tombs both pre-dated and post-dated the second or final stage of the monument, showing the longevity of tomb building that was carried on at Knowth. The modelling of over 60 radiocarbon dates, which were primarily on human bone from the various tombs across the site, indicates that the main use occurred between 3200 and 2900 BC, essentially lasting a minimum of about 100 to 220 years but, at a maximum, up to 300 years. This meant that human remains were being deposited in these tombs spanning at least three to five generations, but potentially up to as many as nine or ten generations (Cooney 2017; Schulting *et al.* 2017).

Furthermore, when George Eogan took a closer look at the megalithic art, he noticed that some stones with distinctive spiral and zigzag patterns appeared to be reused or recycled stones, some of which had been built into the first stage of the large mound (see Chapter 5). This led to the suggestion that another passage tomb, at least one but maybe more, had been dismantled and its stones reused. Although no other archaeological evidence was recovered for this so-called 'Tomb 1A', it is possible that it remains preserved underneath the unexcavated portion of the mound.

If we take a closer look at that first phase of the large mound (Tomb 1B), it can be seen that the east and the west tombs were separated by a distance of just under four metres. It is likely that they were built at the same time, with the associated stone cairn constructed around them, acting, essentially, like scaffolding, particularly when it came to constructing the elaborate corbelled roof of the eastern chamber, which stands at just over six metres in height internally.

The stone cairn itself, which is estimated to be over 40 metres in diameter, also appears

to have been splayed at the entrances, creating a sort of formal V-shaped approach to both tombs in this first phase of building.

ENLARGED TOMB

It is unknown how long this first phase of the tomb stood before the people decided to go back and enlarge it by extending both of the passages. They did this by adding another roughly 24 metres of passage on the east side and 27 metres on the west side. This was a huge undertaking considering that it meant

Above: **The splayed entrance to the east passage of Tomb 1B, as uncovered during excavation.**

Right: **Extended west passage that enlarged the monument into Tomb 1C.**

What Lies Beneath: Uncovering the Story of Knowth Through Time

potentially sourcing an additional 140 orthostats or upright stones, 85 capstones or lintels and potentially over 60 corbels, which would have been positioned between the orthostats and the capstones to create a level passage roof. Furthermore, building the encompassing mound must have been a highly organized and ritualized act, whereby very distinctive layers of re-deposited sods, boulder clay, shale, water-rolled and quarried stones were all laid down in sequence around this now huge tomb. A further 127 stones were selected as kerbstones and added around the base of the mound, covering a circumference of some 300 metres.

The new entrances to both passages were also elaborately emphasized by adding decorated kerbstones, stone settings and deposits of quartz, granite and banded stones. These stones were carefully selected with size, shape, colour and texture all influencing factors in deciding which stones were included in these areas of display. Many of them came from quite far away, with the granodiorite and the banded siltstones likely coming from as far north as Dundalk Bay, some 40 kilometres away, while the quartz may have come from Rockabill Island off the coast near Skerries in north Dublin (Corcoran and Sevastopulo 2017). These would have been transported by boat to the mouth of the Boyne before travelling on upriver to Brú na Bóinne.

The entrance settings also included prominent standing stones, which mark the axes of the passages externally. Both stones were chosen for very different reasons; that outside the west tomb is a smooth red sandstone, while that outside the east tomb is a rough limestone block with a vertical rib of chert.

ARTEFACTS

Besides the wonderful array of megalithic art (Shee Twohig 2022), the passage tombs are probably most famous for their associated artefacts. In the western tomb of the large mound, this included a beautiful gabbro macehead, pins manufactured from antler and a sandstone (greywacke) basin stone. The basin originally would have sat in the chamber area just inside the outer sill stone where a depression was evident in the ground. At some time in the past, however, an effort was made to try to remove it. It appears as if somebody attempted to roll it up the passage and in doing so considerably damaged the basin, to the point where the edges are now quite rough. It must, however, have been too much effort and they decided to abandon the heist, leaving the basin stone sitting on the floor of the passage where it remains to this day.

In the eastern tomb, a selection of pin fragments was also recovered, again made from antler but also some pig bones, as well as several pendants and beads made from stone, antler and fired clay. Many of these can be interpreted as representing miniature versions of larger objects such as pestle hammers or maceheads, as well as two very special knobbed beads that are miniature versions of carved stone balls, a type of artefact that is primarily known from Scotland (see Chapter 6). The flint macehead and the decorated granite basin

---

Opposite page: **Looking into the north (right-hand) recess of the east tomb with the basin stone sitting behind two free-standing jamb stones at the entrance.**

What Lies Beneath? Uncovering the Story of Knowth Through Time

stone, which probably represent two of the most iconic discoveries from the site, were also found in the eastern tomb (see Chapter 5).

Above: **Artefacts from the eastern tomb included pendants and beads.**

Notably, the recess in which the granite basin was placed may have been built around it. The basin certainly had to have been in position before the two large, free-standing pillars or jamb stones were placed in front of the recess. Equally intriguing is that small deposits of cremated bone in shallow scoops were found underneath the basin, suggesting that the addition of human remains to the tomb may have been taking place from a very early stage in its construction.

Another interesting discovery in the east chamber came from the opposite recess. This was a cattle scapula that had been cut along one side of the central ridge. There was also evidence for wear along the broad face of the bone on one side. This is often interpreted as a shovel-like implement and it could have been used to carry cremated bone into the chamber, after which it was intentionally left there, placed on a layer of shale stones within and underneath a large deposit of cremated human bone.

Examination of the burial deposits found in all the tombs at Knowth suggests that over 270 individuals may have been laid to rest there, of which over 200 were cremated and the rest deposited as unburnt remains (Buckley *et al.* 2017). This practice of including fragmented non-burnt bones along with cremated bone is now evident at many Irish passage tombs and furthers the argument that the people using these monuments were engaged in quite complex mortuary rites. This likely included both cremating whole bodies soon after death, while excarnating and disarticulating other bodies, allowing for bones to be retained and circulated, as well as the cremation of dry bone. With this in mind, it might also be argued that the estimates of the number of dead at Knowth should be reconsidered. Many of the small fragments of non-burnt bone could have come from the same individuals as the cremated bone. This would, for example, reduce the number of people interred in the eastern tomb to 131 rather than 178 (Cooney 2017).

CONTINUED DEPOSITION

From about 3000/2900 BC, following this initial zenith of tomb building, ceremonial and burial practices, the passage tomb cemetery remained very much an important place on the landscape. Associated rituals now incorporated another new style of pottery known as Grooved Ware, which had developed on the Orkney Islands a century or so earlier.

One such ritual was the placing of a Grooved Ware pot into the chamber of Tomb 6. It was long suggested that this vessel represented an early style of this ceramic type (Brindley 1999, Sheridan 2004). Many years later, radiocarbon dating of both cremated and non-burnt human bone from Tomb 6 confirmed this. A desire to continue this tradition of placing human remains within the tombs was evident also in stratigraphically later deposits of bone found in Tombs 15 and 17, as well as placed into the outer part of the western passage of the large mound.

The latter was particularly intriguing as the bone was placed behind one of the passage orthostats. While it may be that people added it as the mound was being built, it is perhaps more likely that the corbel, which once sat on top of the orthostat, had slipped backwards into the mound, pushing the orthostat forward slightly and creating a gap that allowed somebody to reach in and place a small offering of cremated human bone.

This continued use of the site is also represented by the construction of a timber circle outside the eastern entrance into the large mound sometime around 2700–2500 BC. The remains of over 50 Grooved Ware pots were found in association with this monument, as well as worked flint, a stone axehead, animal bone representing cattle and pig, and charred wheat, barley and hazelnut shell. The entrances to many of the tombs were also re-emphasized at this time. This practice also continued for several more centuries as deposits of Beaker pottery and associated occupation material suggest the site remained an important place, perhaps even a place of pilgrimage.

Nearly 100 Beaker-style vessels were recovered during the excavations at Knowth and these were found alongside hearths, pits, some post-holes and occupation refuse that included worked flint and knapping debris, small amounts of cattle and pig bone and charred seeds and grains representing plants like wheat, bramble, thistle and buttercup. In many places, these clusters of Beaker material overlay the Grooved Ware deposits. It has been suggested (Carlin 2018) that these locations of deposition were intentionally selected to reference particular aspects of the earlier passage tombs, such as the entrances to Tombs 2, 6, 15 and 20, as well as the east passage of the large mound where the timber circle had been built.

From about 2200 BC onwards until the Late Iron Age, around 100 BC, a period of some two millennia, activity at Knowth seems to have significantly decreased or at least remained largely undetectable in the archaeological record. Three pottery vessels, the tip of a bronze sickle and a radiocarbon date suggest some visitors may have come to the site around 1500 BC or slightly later. It can be speculated that during this time the site may have returned to agricultural land, switching from a place of gathering and ceremony back to a place where animals grazed and crops were grown.

RENEWED ACTIVITY

From about 100 BC to around AD 300, Knowth was used once again for burial when the

Above: **Displaced corbel 5/6 and orthostat 5 in the western passage of the large mound, behind which human bone was placed in the Late Neolithic.**

Opposite page: **The presence of Beaker pottery showed that Knowth remained an important site in the Chalcolithic period.**

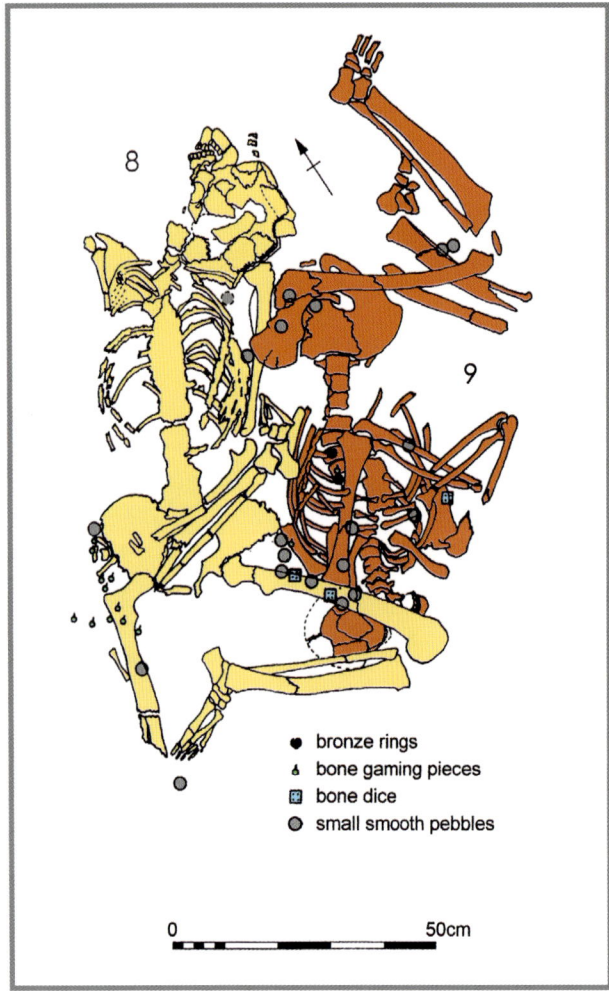

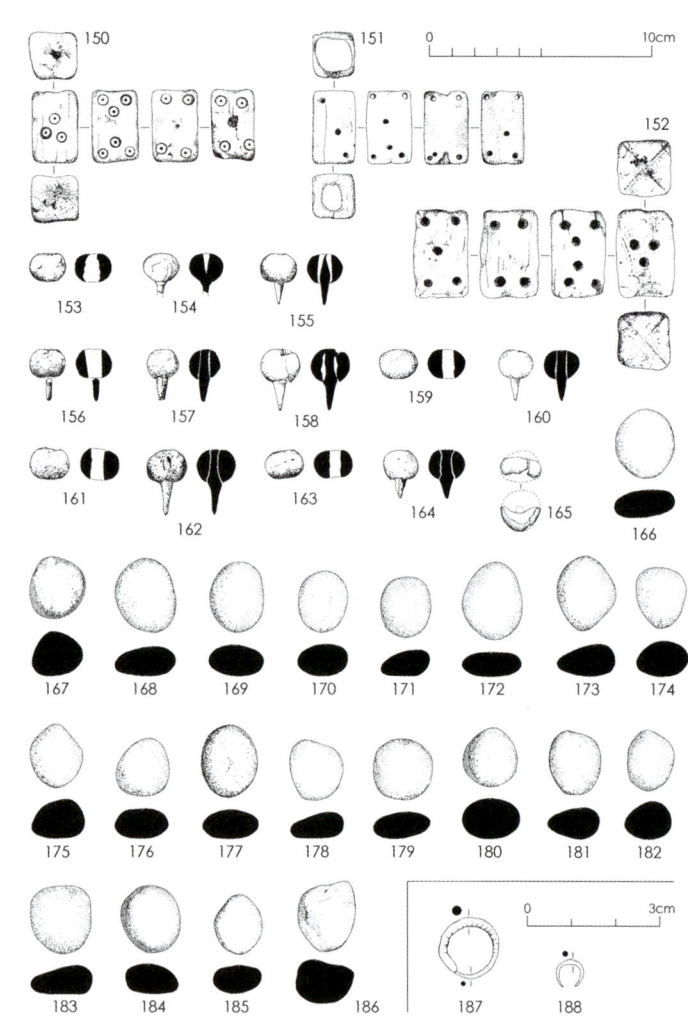

Above: The burial placement of 'The Gamblers' with their accompanying gaming pieces, from the Late Iron Age.

Opposite page: Artist's impression of Knowth in the Early Medieval period when the mound was altered into a stepped shape with (left) a causeway leading to the top.

remains of at least 14 but possibly as many as 20 individuals were placed in graves that were dug into the passage tomb mounds, as well as placed into the interiors of Tombs 2, 9 and 15. Most of these burials were flexed or crouched and several were accompanied by objects such as copper-alloy rings, glass and bone beads and what are usually referred to as gaming pieces. It has been suggested that the earliest of these burials may represent people who had recently moved into the area, with their style of burial reflecting influence from Britain in the pre-Roman or early post-conquest period (O'Brien 2020).

One of the most famous of the burials from this time became known as 'The Gamblers' due to the accompanying bone dice, pegs and smooth stone counters. These two adult males were placed head to toe and they were recorded as being roughly of the same age and height. They had also very similar strontium and oxygen isotope results and this led to suggestions that they likely originated in northern Britain (Cahill-Wilson *et al.* 2012). It has also been speculated that they may have been brothers, perhaps even twins, and possibly healers or druids that used divination or occult practices, as suggested by the objects that were buried with them.

DESTRUCTION AND CHANGE

The next major identifiable phase at Knowth took place between the fifth and ninth centuries AD. This began with the burial of a further 14 individuals across the site, this time as extended inhumations, with some placed in stoned-lined graves. It has been suggested that these new burials represented the royal lineage of what would ultimately develop into the seat of the kings of Northern Brega (Gleeson 2018).

This was the first time also that there was definite evidence for the destruction and alteration of some of the earlier passage tombs. This included adding Insular script and ogham to some of the structural stones within the large mound, sometimes on top of or slightly overlapping the much earlier megalithic art. It also involved converting the large mound into what has been termed a 'double-ditched enclosure', which was really more of a stepped mound, with access to the top via a steep

causeway on the south-eastern side.

The large outer ditch was placed directly behind the kerbstones that defined the base of the passage tomb mound. It has always been a source of amazement that more damage was not done at this time to the kerbstones, many of which are highly decorated. This ditch, however, did result in the removal of between four to five metres from the outer part of the east and west passages, meaning that any stratigraphical relationship between the entrance kerbstones and the passages was lost at this time.

Choosing an ancient monument as a site for legitimizing and establishing one's right to kingship or leadership is long attested, including at places like Tara, and it has been suggested that Knowth may have been a place of assembly at this time, perhaps even one of inauguration. It was also likely linked to a nearby secular cemetery site to the north-east, where excavations undertaken in the early 2000s, by Geraldine and Matthew Stout (Stout and Stout 2008), uncovered a stone-lined grave that incorporated some megalithic art. It is not unreasonable, then, to think that this stone slab was taken from Knowth at a time when the large mound was being remodelled and some of the smaller tombs were being partially dismantled.

Knowth continued to be transformed between the ninth and eleventh centuries AD when it developed into a focus for settlement and craftworking. The remains of at least 14 rectangular buildings were uncovered, as well

Right: **The outer passages of the large mound were re-aligned to link with later souterrains.**

What Lies Beneath? Uncovering the Story of Knowth Through Time

as nine souterrains or underground structures, and various areas dedicated to iron smelting, bronze- and gold-working and enamelling. Knowth really flourished during this time, with the excavations revealing evidence also for its important external contacts, mostly likely via the two main Viking coastal centres of Dublin to the south and Annagassan, County Louth, to the north.

By now, the large mound and much of the surrounding area were utterly transformed, with many of the smaller passage tombs extensively damaged. This is best illustrated by the re-use of stones with megalithic art in the construction of the new houses and souterrains, as well as the realignment of the outer ends of the east and west passages of the large mound. This was done in order to directly link them to the houses and some of the souterrains, one of which extended right up into the mound, roughly parallel to the eastern passage.

People at this time also reused the chamber of the eastern tomb, as evidenced by the discovery of hearths, pits and stone paving, as well as various artefacts such as ring-headed pins, beads of glass, amber and stone, jet or lignite bangles, an amber finger-ring and a copper-alloy bell pendant. It has been suggested that some of these items could have been strung together as a single necklace (Ó Floinn 2012). So the question remains, did it break while somebody was in the chamber, where it was too dark for them to collect their lost items, or were a necklace and other objects left intentionally in a place that was now viewed simply as another souterrain, a place for safely storing personal items?

Alternatively, could the inner chamber of

the Neolithic passage tomb still have been recognized as sacred? Much like caves, some tombs were certainly seen as places of the Otherworld during this time (Dowd 2015) and Knowth may have been one such site.

MEDIEVAL AND LATER

By the eleventh century, the kingdom of North Brega was in decline and, in 1157, it was granted to the Cistercian order of monks. After this, the large mound was remodelled again, including the addition of ditches, a bastion and a levelling layer on the summit. The latter was in preparation for the building of an enclosed courtyard farm in the fourteenth century. Although little of this actually survived due to the later quarrying mentioned earlier, there was some evidence for a stone-built wall, at least two structures and some paving. This has been interpreted as the remains of a secular farm that may have been built by the holder of land leased from the Cistercians at this time (O'Keeffe 2012).

The Reformation in the sixteenth century brought additional changes and by the 1640s the old landowning families in the area had been largely dispossessed of their properties. In contrast to earlier centuries, seventeenth- and eighteenth-century settlement at Knowth was confined to the areas surrounding the large mound rather than on the mound itself. By this time, little trace of the smaller tombs survived. Additional houses were built on the opposite side of the public road to Knowth, probably representing the homes of the labouring families that worked this farmland, which by now was part of the Caldwell estate. Around 1840, these buildings were replaced by Robinson's farmhouse, yard and outbuildings which, of course, still stand at the site today.

THE KNOWTH LEGACY

It is fair to say that what lay beneath the grass-covered mound that George Eogan started working on in 1962 greatly added to and sometimes even changed our understanding of Irish archaeology, not just for the Neolithic but across several time periods. The legacy of the Knowth project includes transforming our understanding of passage tomb building and its associated rituals. It includes how human remains and objects were treated and deposited in complex ways, and how communities continued to engage with these monuments long after they had been built, with Grooved Ware and Beaker-using people returning to the site again and again, perhaps

Right: **George Eogan and members of the excavation team, including Fiona Eogan, working at the west tomb in 1967.**

Opposite page: **The summit of the large mound was levelled in the Late Medieval period to support a stone wall and farm buildings.**

to take part in communal gatherings and feastings.

The archaeology of the ninth to twelfth-century layers also has greatly influenced our understanding of rural settlement at the time, with the associated animal bone assemblage representing one of the largest ever excavated in Ireland. Analysis of the remains from this period led to the suggestion that there was a move away from an economic value system based on livestock, especially cow milk, to one where slaves and silver played an increasingly important role (McCormick and Murray 2007).

The archaeology is just one aspect of the legacy of Knowth, however; there is also a wider societal impact. As the excavations were carried on seasonally for 38 years, sometimes for up to four months at a time, the staff were the backbone of the project. This included a mix of local labour, students, archaeologists and specialists, many of whom returned to the site year after year and developed friendships that long outlasted the excavations. Furthermore, the discoveries have also formed the basis of inspiration for many songwriters, poets, visual artists, jewellery makers and others. This creativity has been influenced by the megalithic art motifs, the carefully manufactured artefacts and the overall ambiance of Knowth as a sacred place – a place with shadows of the past.

Acknowledgements

I am very much just one person in an exceptionally large number of people who have worked both at Knowth and on the Knowth material over many years, all of whom have greatly contributed to the story of the site.

The seven volumes in the *Excavations at Knowth* series, published by the Royal Irish Academy, begun in 1984 and finished with the last volume early in 2022, comprise over 3,500 pages by 100 named contributors. They demonstrate the multidisciplinary and collaborative nature of the Knowth project from the beginning.

I want to acknowledge the unwavering support that the Knowth project has received over the years from many different people and institutions. Chief among them are the Royal Irish Academy, the UCD School of Archaeology, the Heritage Council of Ireland, Office of Public Works, the National Monuments Service and the National Museum of Ireland.

I am also very much indebted to the photographic work of Ken Williams, who has brought Knowth to life through his images over the years, and to artist Steve Doogan for his beautiful reconstruction drawings of the site. Finally, I thank Helena King and Ruth Hegarty of the Royal Irish Academy, as well as Fiona, James and all the Eogan family for their support throughout the years of working on the Knowth material. It remains a privilege.

BIBLIOGRAPHY

Brindley, A.L. 1999. Irish Grooved Ware *IN*: Cleal, R. and MacSween, A. (eds.) *Grooved Ware in Britain and Ireland*, Neolithic Studies Group Seminar Papers 3. Oxford: Oxbow Books. pp23–55.

Buckley, L., Power, C., O'Sullivan, R. and Thakore, H. 2017. The human remains *IN*: Eogan, G. and Cleary, K. (eds.) *Excavations at Knowth 6: The Passage Tomb Archaeology of the Great Mound at*

Knowth. Dublin: Royal Irish Academy. pp277–329.

Cahill-Wilson, J., Usborne, H., Taylor, C., Ditchfield, P. and Pike, A.W.G. 2012. Strontium and oxygen isotope analysis on Iron Age and Early Historic burials around the Great Mound *IN:* Eogan, G. *Excavations at Knowth 5: The Archaeology of Knowth in the First and Second Millennia AD*. Dublin: Royal Irish Academy. pp775–87.

Carlin, N. 2018. *The Beaker Phenomenon? Understanding the character and context of social practices in Ireland 2500-2000 BC*. Leiden: Sidestone Press.

Cooney, G. 2017. The Knowth mortuary practices in context *IN:* Eogan, G. and Cleary, K. (eds.) *Excavations at Knowth 6: The Passage Tomb Archaeology of the Great Mound at Knowth*. Dublin: Royal Irish Academy. pp387–410.

Corcoran, M. and Sevastopulo, G. 2017. Provenance of the stone used in the construction and decoration of Tomb 1 *IN:* Eogan, G. and Cleary, K. (eds.) *Excavations at Knowth 6: The Passage Tomb Archaeology of the Great Mound at Knowth*. Dublin: Royal Irish Academy. pp505–68.

Davis, S. 2017. Insect remains *IN:* Eogan, G. and Cleary, K. (ed.) *Excavations at Knowth 6: The Passage Tomb Archaeology of the Great Mound at Knowth*. Dublin: Royal Irish Academy. pp618–30.

Dowd, M. 2015. *The Archaeology of Caves in Ireland*. Oxford: Oxbow Books.

Gleeson, P. 2018. Gathering communities: locality, governance and rulership in early medieval Ireland. *World Archaeology* 50 (1), pp100–120.

Herity, M. 1967. From Lhuyd to Coffey: new information from unpublished descriptions of the Boyne Valley tombs. *Studia Hibernica* 7. pp127–45.

McCormick, F. and Murray, E. 2007. *Excavations at Knowth 3: Knowth and the Zooarchaeology of Early Christian Ireland*. Dublin: Royal Irish Academy. p112.

O'Brien, E. 2020. *Mapping Death: Burial in Late Iron Age and Early Medieval Ireland*. Dublin: Four Courts Press. p37.

Ó Floinn, R. 2012. Finds from the Knowth excavations: Introduction *IN:* Eogan, G. *Excavations at Knowth 5: The Archaeology of Knowth in the First and Second Millennia AD*. Dublin: Royal Irish Academy. pp225–7.

O'Keeffe, T. 2012. Medieval architectural pieces *IN:* Eogan, G. *Excavations at Knowth 5: The Archaeology of Knowth in the First and Second Millennia AD*. Dublin: Royal Irish Academy. pp619–26.

Shee Twohig, E. 2022. Techniques and Motifs of Knowth Art *IN:* Eogan, G. and Shee Twohig, E. 2022. *Excavations at Knowth 7: The Megalithic Art of the Passage Tombs at Knowth, County Meath*. Dublin: Royal Irish Academy, pp61–123.

Sheridan, J.A. 2004. Going round in circles? Understanding the Irish 'Grooved Ware complex' in its wider context *IN:* Roche, H., Grogan, E., Bradley, J., Coles, J. and Raftery, B. (eds.) *From Megaliths to Metals: Essays in honour of George Eogan*. Oxford: Oxbow Books. pp26–37.

Schulting, R., Bronk Ramsey, C., Reimer, P., Eogan, G., Cleary, K., Cooney, G. and Sheridan, A. 2017. Dating the Neolithic human remains at Knowth *IN:* Eogan, G. and Cleary, K. (eds.) *Excavations at Knowth 6: The Passage Tomb Archaeology of the Great Mound at Knowth*. Dublin: Royal Irish Academy. pp331–79.

Stout, G. and Stout, M. 2008. Excavation of a secular cemetery at Knowth Site M, County Meath, and related sites in north-east Leinster. Dublin: Wordwell.

Chapter 2:

Definitely on more than one occasion, when we were digging at Dowth Hall, when we would be scratching our heads about something, inevitably a voice on the team would pop up, 'I wonder what George would do in this situation.'

DR CLÍODHNA NÍ LIONÁIN

Exploring the Life Cycle of a Forgotten Monument: The Dowth Hall Passage Tomb Excavation

At Brú na Bóinne there is no end to the surprises still in store and the secrets still to be discovered. Dr Clíodhna Ní Lionáin recounts the uncovering of one such secret, the excavation of the recently-discovered passage tomb at Dowth Hall, which she directed, and considers the process whereby some monuments come to be remembered and some slip from public memory entirely.

In 2017, a lost and forgotten monument was rediscovered at Dowth Hall, Co. Meath. Beneath the shadow of this neo-classical Georgian villa lay a large passage tomb (ME020-098— —) waiting to be found. The excavation, which arose from a planning permission condition,

Right: The surviving interior of tomb 1 of Dowth Hall passage tomb.

Exploring the Life Cycle of a Forgotten Monument: the Dowth Hall Passage Tomb Excavation

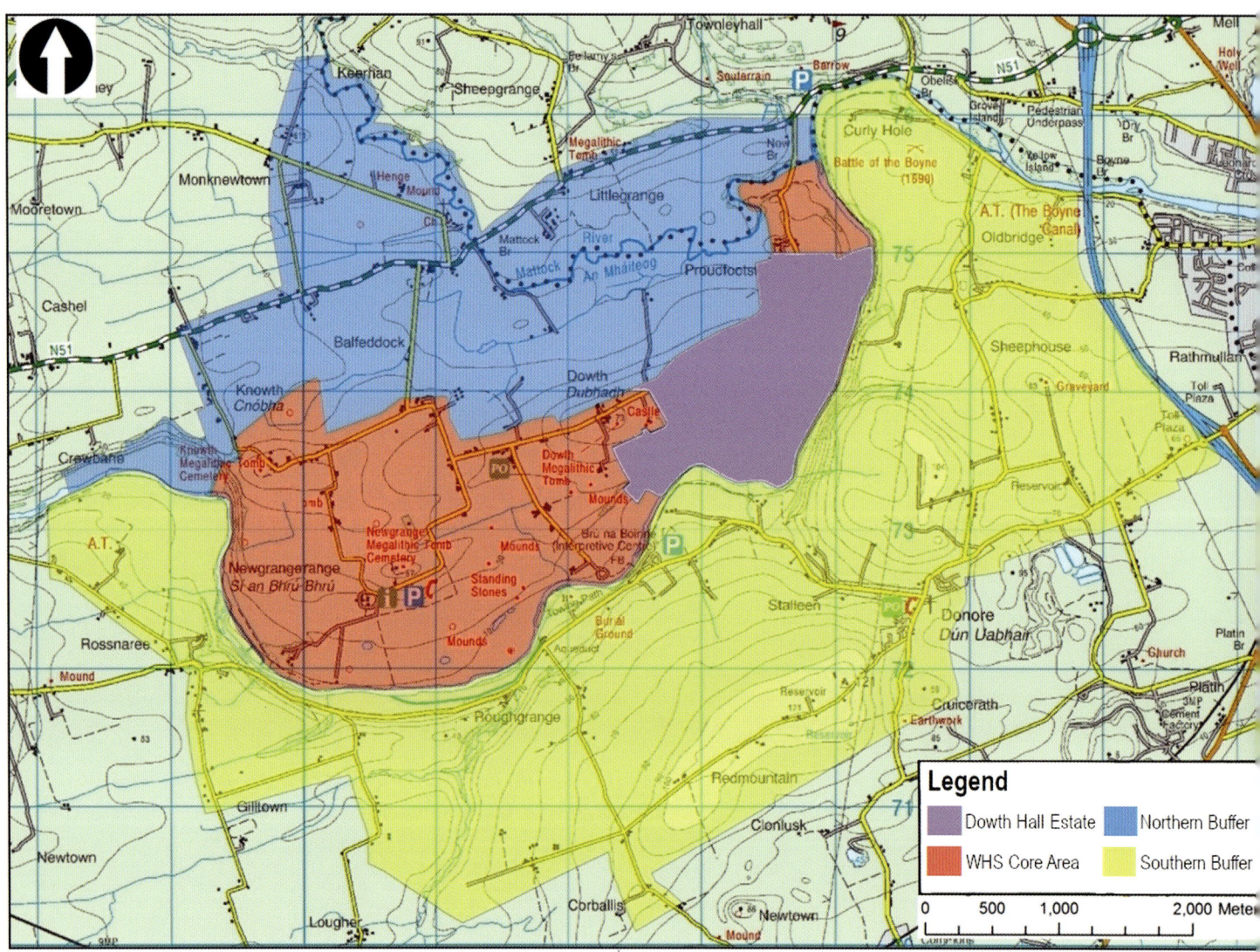

was undertaken over three phases, totalling nearly twenty-one months. It was fully funded by the landowners, Devenish, and undertaken in collaboration with UCD School of Archaeology. Throughout the excavation, the voices of the people who came before us – from the Neolithic tomb builders to the modern excavators of other passage tombs in the area – were ever present as we worked to rediscover this monument. In particular, the work of Prof. Eogan and his team at Knowth created a unique and comprehensive resource for the archaeological community that proved invaluable.

Located *c.*7km east of Slane, the passage tomb is on the estate associated with Dowth Hall. At more than 430 acres in size, the estate represents a fifth of the core area of the UNESCO World Heritage Site of Brú na Bóinne. The passage tomb is situated at the eastern end of a shale ridge that was the focus of significant ritual activity in the Neolithic.

Three fields to the west of the Dowth Hall passage tomb lies the large, state-owned passage tomb at Dowth (ME020-017——), which is approximately twice the size of the former. Originally, both monuments formed part of the same estate but Dowth has been under state ownership since 1997. Further west, there are two other mega-mounds at Newgrange (ME019-045——) and Knowth (ME019-030001-). Although smaller in size, the Dowth Hall passage tomb could be considered part of this phenomenon of building large focal monuments. Of note is the comparability in size of an earlier iteration of the Knowth monument, Tomb 1B, *c.*38m diameter, (Eogan and Cleary 2017, 137)) and the dimensions of the Dowth Hall passage tomb (*c.*40m diameter).

MEMORIES OF NEARBY MONUMENTS

Before discussing the details of the excavation, this paper will look at the archaeological sites and architectural structures in the immediate vicinity to explore how some monuments are remembered while others are forgotten. The closest example is Dowth Hall itself, the construction of which began in the 1740s and was completed around 1765. However, the earliest depictions of the house are black-and-white interior photographs from 1915 (Sadleir and Dickenson 1915). To date, no earlier sketches, watercolours or even the architectural plans have been found. While this house is still very visible and is physically within our current cultural landscape, there are still quite a few gaps in our collective memory about it.

Around 325m to the north-east of Dowth Hall, Dowth Henge (ME020-010——) is located at the easternmost end of the shale ridge. This Late Neolithic embanked enclosure is the second-largest henge on the island of

Below: One of the earliest images of Dowth Hall, a photograph of the drawing room from 1915.

Opposite page: Map of the UNESCO World Heritage Site of the Bend of the Boyne, showing location of Dowth Hall estate. The core area is shown in pink and the estate in lilac.

Ireland, second only to Ballynahatty or the Giant's Ring outside Belfast. When looking through its western entrance, it appears to be aligned on Dowth Hall or, rather, on the passage tomb that lies beneath it. Dowth Henge is still very monumental and visible in our landscape, with its banks surviving up to six metres high in places. It may also have formed the backdrop against which some early Irish myths and legends played out, in particular a story called *Fled Dúin na nGéd* or 'The Banquet of the Fort of the Geese'. According to this tale, a high king of Ireland, King Domhnall, wanted to celebrate the construction of his new palace by hosting a lavish feast. He requested that all the goose eggs in Ireland be brought to the feast. Some of his followers headed down the road to Slane, where they came across the hermitage of Bishop Erc, who was not at home. They entered and found a vessel full of goose eggs, which they stole, leading Erc to curse the banquet. At the feast, King Domhnall had an argument with his foster son, Congal Caech, the king of Ulster, which ultimately led to the Battle of Magh Rath (*Cath Muighe Rath*) in 637 AD.

In his translations in 1842, John O'Donovan, the Irish language scholar, presented the banquet story as a prequel to the battle. In one of the footnotes, while acknowledging that none of the local people in the area remembered the place name of *Dún na nGéd*, he suggested that the story was probably referring to a large fort near Dowth on the southern side of the Boyne River (O'Donovan 1842, 6). However, in 1850, the antiquarian Sir William Wilde specifically identified the site of the banquet as Dowth Henge (Wilde,

Above: **Dowth passage tomb in 1775, painted by the Dutch artist Gabriel Beranger.**

Opposite page: **Aerial photograph (© OSI) of Dowth Hall and its environs, showing Dowth Henge, the passage tombs at Sites I and J, and Dowth passage tomb.**

1850, 211). It is not clear if this attribution to Dowth Henge is a nineteenth-century invention or if it has roots in an older tradition but it shows how these legends and tales can end up being connected to monuments that are still physically visible and present in the contemporary cultural landscape.

On the lawn to the west of Dowth Hall, there are two small mounds (ME020-012——; ME020-013——), both of which appear to be passage tombs. They were known about and discussed since at least the nineteenth century, when the scholar and archaeologist George Coffey labelled them as Site I and Site J respectively in his recording system for monuments in the area (Smyth 2009, 14). Prior to this, they were depicted in the first edition Ordnance Survey of 1836, when Site J (ME020-013——) was labelled as a 'cave'. The use of this misnomer suggests that the chamber capstone had already been removed by this point.

Located around 640m west of Dowth Hall, the state-owned passage tomb at Dowth (ME020-017—-) is still very imposing and has been remembered in a variety of different ways. In 1775, the artist Gabriel Beranger painted a beautiful watercolour of it. During that same visit, he painted a possible stone circle (ME020-009——, Cloghalea) to the north-east of Dowth Henge, which is no longer visible. Unfortunately, by the time of his visit, Dowth Hall was already a decade old, so the passage tomb underneath would not have been visible to him. There are also much older references to the passage tomb at Dowth (ME020-017——) in our historic sources. An entry in the *Annals of Ulster* describes an event in AD 863 when the Vikings, probably from Dublin, sailed up the Boyne and attacked a series of mounds or caves, including that of 'Boadan's mound above Dubad' [Dowth] (MacAirt and MacNiocaill 1983, 319).

This brief overview of the immediate vicinity of the Dowth Hall passage tomb shows the different ways that monuments and structures can be remembered – through the legends and myths that develop around them, through illustrations or cartographic representations, or through local folklore and knowledge. However, for some reason, the Dowth Hall passage tomb was not remem-

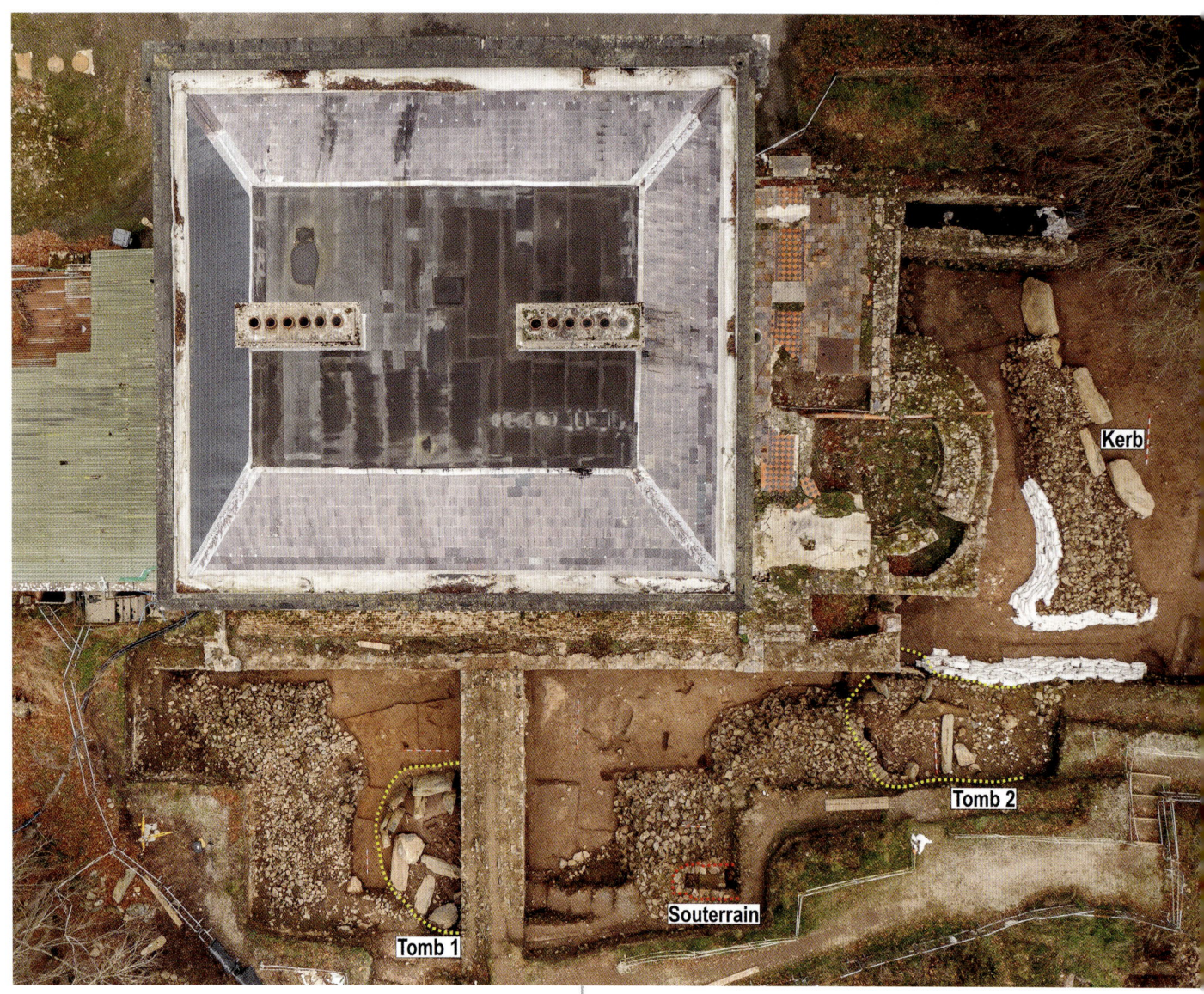

Above: **Aerial photo of the Dowth Hall passage tomb showing burial chambers (Tombs 1 and 2), the kerb and the souterrain entrance**

bered in any of these ways. Perhaps the excavation of this site can reveal what happened to the passage tomb during its life that caused it to slip so totally into oblivion.

THE NINE PHASES OF ACTIVITY AT DOWTH HALL PASSAGE TOMB	
(1)	Pre-Cairn Activity
(2)	Construction and Use
(?)	Deliberate Decommissioning / Chamber Infill
(4)	Beaker Activity
(5)	Cairn Slippage
(6)	Perimeter Redefinition & Cremation Burial
(7)	Medieval Activity
(8)	18th and 19th Century Building and Landscape
(9)	21st Century Rediscovery and Excavation

THE EXCAVATION OF THE DOWTH HALL PASSAGE TOMB

When excavation started on the Dowth Hall passage tomb in 2017, the first structures that were encountered were associated with the eighteenth-century house, including an external basement that wraps around the outside of the house and is accessed by a series of servants' tunnels. Part of the original southern wing was also discovered and was found to have been more elaborate than originally thought, having a bowed projection (a semi-circular bay).

As the excavation progressed deeper, the vestiges of a much older monument were encountered – the remains of a large passage tomb, measuring about 40 metres in diameter. Significantly damaged over the course of its lifetime, the surviving remains of the passage tomb consisted of two burial chambers in the western side of the mound, a partial kerb (six kerbstones) and a stone cairn surviving to a maximum height of 1.60m. Two of the kerbstones have slipped out of position, while the most easterly kerbstone was incorporated into the nearby servants' tunnel. The covering stone mound or cairn consisted mainly of quarried sandstone, which was subsequently exploited by the eighteenth century builders to provide material for the basement structures. The various interventions on the site have created a jigsaw puzzle with many different layers and episodes of activity to be disentangled and deciphered.

To date, at least eight phases in the life of this monument have been provisionally identified. The earliest phase is pre-cairn activity prior to the construction of the stone elements of the passage tomb. The next phase was the building of the chambers, the kerb and the cairn, and the initial use of the monument. This was followed by a phase of 'deliberate decommissioning' when the chambers appear to have been dismantled intentionally and infilled with stone. This may have taken place during the Chalcolithic but further dating work is required to confirm this. Various episodes of cairn slippage were recorded, some of which preceded evidence of Chalcolithic (Beaker) activity immediately south of the kerb. Subsequent cairn slippage layers were cut by a ditch, the purpose of which may have been to redefine the perimeter of the monument. A cremation burial was also placed into the slippage but it is unclear if it is contemporary with the ditch. The next phase of activity was during the Early Medieval period, when a souterrain was inserted into the monument. Around a

millennia later, Dowth Hall was constructed, which represented the most significant building intervention on the site. The twenty-first century rediscovery and archaeological excavation of the site could be considered the most recent phase of the site. As archaeologists, we often see ourselves as scientific, objective observers but the work we undertake also represents part of the biography of these monuments.

PRE-CAIRN ACTIVITY

Some pits were found underneath the cairn, including two small pits east of the northernmost chamber (Tomb 1). Further south, there

is a larger pit, which contained a charcoal lens, with two smaller pits to the west and south-west of it (Figure 8). These features did not seem to form a structure and in the absence of radiocarbon dates, it is not yet known whether they predate the passage tomb by a significant period of time or are broadly contemporaneous.

The most significant layer of pre-cairn activity was the deposition of multiple grass sod layers or turves under the entire footprint of the cairn. They appear to represent site preparation and should be considered part of the construction process (Figure 9). At least

Above left: **(Fig 9)** Buried grass sod layers to the east of Tomb 1, with imprint of cairn stones still visible.

Above right: **(Fig 10)** Aerial view of Tomb 1 showing stalls A, B and C, collapsed structural stones (T1.8-T1.12), and possible stone setting.

Opposite page: **(Fig 8)** Aerial view of pits (outlined in white) that were sealed by the buried grass sod layers underneath the cairn.

four or five turve lines were visible to the naked eye. The logistical implications of depositing these sod layers would have been significant both in terms of excavating and transporting the required quantity of sods to site. This activity also would have had a huge visual impact on the landscape of the donor sites.

CONSTRUCTION AND USE OF TOMB 1

Most of the northernmost burial chamber (Tomb 1) was excavated. Significant damage had been caused during the eighteenth century, as evidenced by the close proximity of a servants' tunnel immediately south of the chamber (Figure 10). However, seven orthostats/uprights were still *in situ* in the eastern part of the chamber where they formed three stalls. A possible angular stone setting was recorded in the central chamber area, where two stones were found at right angles to each other. This possible setting was not exposed fully as its potential western extent is underneath a stone layer that runs under some collapsed structural stones. One of these collapsed structural stones (T1.12) probably formed the western side of Stall C. It is underneath a sub-circular-shaped stone (T1.11) that may have been the roof stone for that stall (Figure 10, outlined in red). Further southwest, there is another very similarly shaped stone (T1.10) that could have been a roof stone for the passage. Immediately east of it (Figure 10) there is a possible lintel (T1.8) that could originally have spanned the passage.

One of the collapsed orthostats (T1.9) is decorated with a large, stacked chevron motif that occupies the upper third of the stone

Top: **(Fig 12)** Stone concretions deposited on the floor of Stall A (Tomb 1).

Above: **(Fig 13)** Stone floor in Stall B that sealed a bone-rich layer. Composite photo showing collapsed orthostat in original upright position.

Opposite page: **(Fig 11)** Stacked chevron motif on T1.9.

(Figure 11). The scale of the motif and the location of the orthostat could suggest that it marked a place of transition, such as the boundary between the passage and chamber, with comparable 'guardian stones' found in other passage tombs. In total, five of the orthostats in Tomb 1 are decorated, employing a mix of pecked and lightly incised motifs.

The excavation of the original chamber deposits showed that Stalls A and B were treated in quite different ways. In Stall A (Figure 12) more than 130 stone balls were pressed into the sticky clay floor. These stone balls were not carved but instead are naturally occurring concretions within sandstone. During the formation process of sandstone, concretions can form around small pieces of grit or a fossil. When the passage tomb builders were quarrying the sandstone to build their cairn, they obviously came across these little oddities, put them to one side (i.e., curated them), and when the chamber was completed they deposited them as ritual objects.

Stall B, immediately north of Stall A, was treated in a completely different way (Figure 13). In Stall B, a bone-rich layer of soil was deposited directly onto the chamber floor, which was then sealed with a stone surface/floor, upon which more cremated bone was deposited.

Left: **(Fig 14) Aerial photograph of Tomb 2, showing side chamber (red) and ramp (white) with orthostats highlighted in colour and the modern tunnel wall on the top right.**

Opposite page: **(Fig 15) Horizontal orthostat (T2.9) resting on vertical stone/prop within Tomb 2 side chamber.**

As well as cremated bone, unburnt human remains were also found in Tomb 1, including two fragments of a mandible that were deposited either side of the southern stone of the central stone setting. It appears that the mandible fragments belonged to the same individual – an adult female *c.*17–25 years (Keating 2021, 8). The mandible was dated to between 3191 and 3009 cal BC, 2 sigma (Ní Lionáin 2021, 4), which is well within the main period of use for Knowth and Newgrange. It, and the other unburnt human remains from Tomb 1, are currently undergoing ancient DNA analysis by Dr Lara Cassidy of Trinity College Dublin (TCD), which should tell us more about the individual, possible family connections, and wider population links.

CONSTRUCTION OF TOMB 2

The southern burial chamber (Tomb 2) is located *c.*16.5 metres south of Tomb 1 and remains mostly unexcavated. A trench was excavated through the cairn immediately east of Tomb 2, which revealed the presence of a side chamber (Figure 14). Though only a small proportion of the side chamber was excavated, it provided insight into its design, construction and possible decommissioning. The first stage in construction was the digging of a foundation trench, which was then lined with the buried grass sod layers. Two orthostats (T2.1, T2.4) were erected along the northern and southern edge of the cut and between them there was a large horizontal stone (T2.9) resting on a smaller vertical stone. Though located immediately west of the external basement, the stratigraphy showed that this stone was already in its horizontal position

Below: **(Fig 16) Aerial view of five kerbstones.**

Opposite page: **Decorated kerbstone (K2).**

prior to the building of Dowth Hall. It could represent a displaced orthostat that was deliberately collapsed, with great care taken to ensure that it fell within a few millimetres of the orthostat to the south of it and on top of a smaller vertical stone. Alternatively, it could have been part of the original design, extending from a drystone rear chamber wall to act as a basin or platform (Fig 15).

The large sandstone slab (T2.3) immediately west of the side chamber and leaning against one of its orthostats is the largest structural stone on the site and one of only two non-greywacke structural stones used by the passage tomb builders. Its underside is covered with cupmarks, some of which seem to form distinct motifs. It could be a capstone that covered the side chamber or formed part of the central chamber roofing.

To the north and outside of the chamber, a possible construction ramp was recorded. Built directly on the buried grass sod layer, the ramp consisted of a layer of small stones sealed by another sod layer. It sloped down towards one of the chamber orthostats (T2.1) and could have been used to help erect the orthostat or support it once it was in place. Like Tomb 1, the location of the passage has not yet been identified but was probably to the south-west or south of the chamber – the presence of an outlier orthostat (T2.8) to the south suggests the latter.

Six kerbstones were found (Figure 16). Three of them are *in situ* and two have fallen out of place, including the most heavily decorated kerbstone, which is covered in concentric circles and spiral designs (K2). The most easterly kerbstone was incorporated into an eighteenth-century servants' tunnel.

DELIBERATE DECOMMISSIONING

A phase of 'Deliberate Decommissioning' appears to have taken place, when at least one of the burial chambers (Tomb 1) was carefully dismantled. Following removal of the modern terrace material in 2017, only the upper parts of the *in situ* orthostats of Tomb 1 were visible, with the chamber interior infilled with stone. During excavation of this stone infill, several collapsed structural stones were uncovered alongside fragments of human remains that appeared to have been deliberately deposited in significant ways. Just outside Stall A, a partial, adult (*c.*17–25 years) female skull was found, consisting of the upper part of the face and the top part of the head (Keating 2021, 10). It had been deposited upside down so that it could act as a container for finger and hand bones, at least some of which belonged to other individuals. Within the skull, there was an adult finger bone, juvenile finger bones belonging to two different infants, and the claw of a small animal (ibid.). This appears to have been a deliberate act, possibly a closing deposit. An adult male mandible was also found further west, deposited on top of the stacked chevron motif of the collapsed orthostat, T1.9. Both the skull (2492–2280 cal BC, 2 sigma) and the mandible (2474–2266 cal BC, 2 sigma) have returned similar Chalcolithic dates (Ní Lionáin 2021, 16).

Could this mean that this act of deliberate decommissioning happened during the Chalcolithic, with contemporary human remains used as closing deposits? Alternatively, the dismantling of the chamber occurred at a later date and it was a coincidence that closely dated Chalcolithic remains were chosen to be deposited in this way. More dating is required, particularly of the animal bone found close to the skull, to determine when this process took place.

CHALCOLITHIC ACTIVITY

Immediately south of the kerb, there was evidence for Chalcolithic activity. Lithics that could be attributed to this period, including a

Above: **View from original ground level, showing kerbstones, surviving cairn material (outlined in white), basement structures, including bowed projection, and southern elevation of Dowth Hall.**

Opposite page: **Post-excavation plan showing cairn, kerbstones and ditch that cut through the cairn slippage.**

petit-tranchet arrowhead, were found in some of the early cairn slippage layers. Above this, and south of kerbstone 5, there was a charcoal-rich layer with frequent pottery inclusions, some of which have been provisionally identified as Beaker. A noticeable reddening of the centre of the vertical face of this kerbstone could be the result of a fire being set against the kerb in the Chalcolithic period.

PERIMETER REDEFINITION AND CREMATION BURIAL

The layer containing Beaker pottery was sealed by more substantial layers of cairn slippage, which were subsequently cut by a ditch that runs east to west across this part of the site. The ditch could represent an attempt to redefine the perimeter of the monument but it is not clear when this took place as no diagnostic or dateable material was recovered from the ditch.

To the north of the ditch, a cremation burial was inserted into the cairn slippage. It consisted of a simple pit, created by the removal of a few stones from the cairn slippage. The pit was filled to the top with cremated bone and then sealed by another stone. It contained nearly 4.5 kgs of burnt bone, representing at least three individuals, two adults and one non-adult, who was an individual surviving to late childhood but aged no older than 17 or 18 years (Keating 2021, 26). The pit has yet to be dated but it post-dates the layers containing Beaker pottery and is presumably prehistoric.

MEDIEVAL ACTIVITY

During the excavation campaign in 2018, the entrance to what appeared to be a souterrain was found *c.*7m north-west of Tomb 2. This rectangular drystone structure was constructed using material from the cairn and a clay layer was deposited on the floor of its interior. At its southern end, there was a step down, but it was not possible to follow the souterrain further as it continued beyond the extent of our excavation. The endpoint of the souterrain was discovered four years later in the latest excavation campaign.

In December 2021, some infill material was excavated along the northern extent of the chamber of Tomb 2, with the aim of

Below: **Entrance to souterrain (discovered in 2018).**

Opposite page: **Souterrain interior viewed from chamber breach point. Roof stone (reused orthostat) visible in upper part of photograph.**

identifying the upper parts of orthostats along the chamber wall. A gap appeared along the centre of the wall, beyond which the interior of the previously discovered souterrain was visible. While souterrains have been recorded in other passage tombs, where they focus on accessing the passage, the Dowth Hall souterrain (ME020-098001) is very unusual in breaching the wall of the chamber itself.

The discovery of the souterrain breach point has the potential to inform our understanding of what the site might have looked like in the Early Medieval Period. The roof stone above the breach point appears to be a chamber orthostat that was flipped into position. This suggests that the site was already a ruin at this stage because it would have been very difficult to tease out the orthostat if the chamber superstructure had been still in place above it. After flipping the orthostat, drystone walling was built over it, as well as over the *in situ* orthostats, which strengthens the argument that this part of the site was open and ruinous at the time. Prior to discovering the souterrain breach point, the drystone walling was interpreted as part of the original corbelling system for the chamber. Following its discovery, it became clear that this 'fake corbelling' had no structural purpose. Perhaps the site was a well-known ruin in the Early Medieval period and the 'fake corbelling' was used to hide the fact that someone had decided to insert a souterrain into it – a case of covering up their tracks. Most of the chamber is still infilled with stone and soil to a depth of at least 1.20

Above: **Excavation of stone infill of Tomb 1, revealing collapsed structural stones ('deliberate decommissioning').**

metres. Without further excavation, it is difficult to assess and understand the full impact of the Early Medieval activity on the site.

DOWTH HALL IN THE MODERN PERIOD

When considering the modern (eighteenth- and nineteenth-century) building interventions, it can be useful to try to imagine what the builders would have seen on their first day on site back in the 1740s. They probably did not come across a fully intact monument but instead one that was very denuded and possibly truncated horizontally. It might have looked like a rocky outcrop with stones peeping out. This theory is informed by the excavation evidence but also by the silence that surrounds this site in antiquarian sources. Despite antiquarians operating in this area for at least 40 years by the time Dowth Hall was constructed, there are no antiquarian references to the presence of a large mound at this site nor any outcry about a mound being destroyed. Knowledge of this site has not been preserved in local history and folklore, which suggests that the site was already a ruin and probably also indicates that the eighteenth-century builders were not drawn from the local community.

LOST MEMORIES

Over time, certain monuments can be forgotten while others are remembered but what was it about the Dowth Hall passage tomb that caused it to be completely forgotten? The seeds of its oblivion were probably planted during the period of deliberate decommissioning, which could have occurred as early as the Chalcolithic. This decommissioning was probably not intended to be a complete obliteration of the site but rather to mark the end of one phase of its life, closing it off to further burials. Regardless of the original intent, the decommissioning was unsuccessful in obliterating it completely because it continued to be remembered over the subsequent millennia until the Early Medieval period at least, when it seems to have still been visible in the cultural landscape of the time, though probably as a ruin.

However, something must have happened between the Early Medieval period and the mid-eighteenth century, when Dowth Hall was built, resulting in the passage tomb completely slipping away from our shared cultural memory. Could it have been that it became so overgrown that the local stories and *piseoga* associated with the site lost the necessary and sustaining link to something tangible and visible, and the site was forgotten? Perhaps it might have been caused or exacerbated by the change of land ownership, coming under the control of an Anglo-Norman family, the Nettervilles. While locals probably still had access, it was perhaps more reduced than it had been prior to them coming into possession. Whatever pushed it over the edge to oblivion, the Dowth Hall passage tomb lay hidden and forgotten for at least 260 years until it entered its most recent phase of life – twenty-first century rediscovery and archaeological excavation, which aims to recover some of the memories of this special site.

Acknowledgements

Many people have contributed to this process of rediscovery, in particular the field crew and the landowners, Devenish, who funded the excavation. Thanks must be given to all those who have been so generous with their time, expertise and skill and those who have included the excavation material in their own research projects – Dr Steve Davis, Dr Helen Lewis, Dr Jessica Smyth, Prof. Gabriel Cooney and Prof. Muiris O'Sullivan of UCD School of Archaeology; Prof. George Sevastopulo, Prof. Patrick Wyse Jackson and Dr Lara Cassidy of Trinity College Dublin; Dr Eimear Meegan and Dr Maurice Murphy of Virtual Lab, Technological University Dublin; Anthony Corns and Rob Shaw of the Discovery Programme; Dr Denise Keating for osteoarchaeological analysis; Ken Williams for site photography and aerial photogrammetry and the Royal Irish Academy for funding for geological thin-sectioning and geochemical analysis. I would like to acknowledge the impact of the work of Professor George Eogan, who we were delighted to welcome to the site with his wife, Fiona, on a number of occasions.

BIBLIOGRAPHY

Eogan, G. and Cleary, K. 2017. *Excavations at Knowth Volume 6: The Passage Tomb Archaeology of the Great Mound at Knowth.* Dublin: Royal Irish Academy, p137.

Keating, D. 2021. *The Human Remains from the Site of Dowth Hall, Co. Meath, 17E0242.* Unpublished report, pp8–11, 26.

MacAirt, S. and MacNiocaill, G. (eds.) 1983. *The Annals of Ulster,* Part 1. Dublin: Dublin Institute for Advanced Studies, p319.

Ní Lionáin, C. 2021. *Preliminary Report (17E0242). Phase 1 Excavation (2021) at Dowth Hall, Co. Meath.* Unpublished report, pp4–6.

O'Donovan, J. 1842. *The banquet of Dun na n-Gedh and the battle of Magh Rath.* Dublin: Irish Archaeological Society, p6.

Sadleir, T.U. and Dickenson, P.L. 1915. *Georgian Mansions in Ireland; With Some Account of the Evolution of Georgian Architecture and Decoration.* Vol. 1. Dublin University Press.

Smyth, J. 2009. *The Brú na Bóinne WHS Research Framework,* p14.

Wilde, W. 1850. *The beauties of the Boyne, and its tributary, the Blackwater.* J. McGlashan, p211.

Chapter 3:

I first met George Eogan in the late 1980s when he was kind enough to allow an over-enthusiastic young one join the excavations at Knowth. He was wonderfully kind. Every time I saw him in subsequent years, he had a kind word and a genuine interest. I remember him with the greatest of fondness and respect.

PROFESSOR JOANNA BRÜCK

Bronze Age Relations: Genetics, Kinship and Gender in Later Prehistory

Professor Joanna Brück is Full Professor of Archaeology at University College Dublin. She has researched and written extensively on the Bronze Age in Britain and in Ireland. In this paper she questions the interpretation of evidence about Bronze Age relations, genetics, kinship and gender from the perspective of modern western cultural norms.

Bronze Age Europe is often viewed as the first globalised economy, a period in which technological innovation and long-distance trade together facilitated the creation of wealth, increasing interpersonal competition and the emergence of institutionalized forms of social difference. According to this evolutionist perspective, the Bronze Age is a stepping stone towards the modern world. Central to the developments of the period, it is argued, were the activities of male warriors, traders and chiefs. Women, in contrast, are viewed as objects of masculine control, displaying the wealth of their husbands in bronze and gold ornaments and traded as wives to bolster the political aspirations of male kin.

This common vision of the Bronze Age foregrounds certain aspects of the evidence such as the appearance of wealthy burials, the development of specialized weapons like swords and rapiers and the accumulation of hoards of scrap metal for recycling and exchange.

It also interprets that evidence from a very particular perspective. Men buried with bronze or gold grave goods are chiefs, traders or craftsmen. Women buried with bronze or gold grave goods are bartered brides. Although it is widely accepted that bronze was not always commodified, even socially significant items exchanged as gifts are viewed primarily as objects to be manipulated in strategies of social and political aggrandizement. Iconographic depictions of Bronze Age warriors, for example on Scandinavian rock art, appear to support this vision of the Bronze Age in which an ideology of competitive individualism underpinned social and economic life.

Quite a different image of the Bronze Age is presented when one examines other aspects of the evidence, however. In Britain, which is my focus in this paper, the expansion of developer-funded archaeology over the past 30 years has reframed our perspec-

Opposite page: Interpretations of the Bronze Age frequently see male warriors and elites as central figures in society, a view that has a long pedigree, as this late 19th-century print demonstrates.

tive away from the hoards and burials that dominated narratives of the Bronze Age for much of the twentieth century. The most common finds now recovered during developer-funded excavations are the residues of everyday life. Some 8,000 settlements of Middle Bronze Age date have now been recorded. The round houses that characterize the architecture of the period in Britain, often part of dense networks of open settlements, field systems, water holes and drove ways scattered across the landscape, present an alternative reading of Bronze Age life in which competition between warrior elites is far from everyday experience and in which women were not devoid of agency but were co-participants in complex social and cultural worlds.

COLONIAL THINKING

In fact, colonial and dualist thinking lies at the heart of accepted narratives. The competitive individualism and economic intensification that are imagined for the Bronze Age are predicated on modes of thinking that are characteristic of the modern western world in which self is divided from other, subject from object, culture from nature, and men from women. In this way, it is possible to see artefacts, women, animals and land as objects to be manipulated and exploited for economic and political gain. But such dualisms are the product of the colonial histories of the recent past. Recent European colonialism was legitimated by figuring land, natural resources and indigenous people as objectified 'others', without history or agency, beyond the bounds of normal social and moral relations. Thus, they could be transformed into commodities to be bought, sold and controlled.

But how do these general comments on the Bronze Age relate to recent advances in archaeogenetics? The potential of ancient DNA to yield extraordinary insights into human mobility, interaction and social structure has been hailed as a scientific revolution. At the beginning of the Bronze Age, the appearance of populations whose genetic ancestry ultimately derived from the Eurasian steppes has been interpreted as indicating the large-scale migration of young men, described by archaeologists as 'war bands', seeking new territories and intermarrying

with local women. These men are viewed as agents of significant social and economic change, introducing new technologies such as metalworking, new modes of transport and intensive exploitation of secondary products.

Beyond the macro level of population genetics, the past few years have also seen increasing numbers of fine-grained analyses of prehistoric burials and cemeteries to understand kinship structures, marriage and residence rules in Bronze Age communities. To date, most of these studies have argued that the primary unit of kinship was the monogamous nuclear family and that patrilineal descent, patrilocal residence and female exogamy, where a woman moves to join her husband on marriage, were the norm. The results of archaeogenetic research, therefore, appear to support views of male-dominated hierarchical Bronze Age societies.

INDIGENOUS CRITIQUES

Before examining the archaeological and genetic evidence for kinship and marriage

Above right: **Sauk family. Nineteenth-century studio portraits like these evocatively demonstrate how Indigenous families were expected to conform to Eurocentric norms.**

Right: **Indian residential school, Fort Resolution, Northwest Territories. European colonial views on family and morality were imposed on Indigenous peoples leading in places to the removal of children from their families into institutions.**

Opposite page: **Reconstruction of the excavated Bronze Age landscape at South Hornchurch, Greater London.**

patterns in the British Bronze Age, it is useful to consider indigenous and anthropological critiques of contemporary western models of kinship, marriage and gender. Indigenous thinkers and other scholars have demonstrated that the imposition of settler sexuality on indigenous communities was a core component of European colonialism in recent centuries. Colonial ideologies defined patriarchal, heteronormative and monogamous family structures as a moral imperative central to the civilizing mission of European settlers.

Children growing up in indigenous families that did not conform to this model were removed to be re-educated in institutions and those whose sexual identity did not fit the dominant binary pattern were shunned, ridiculed and murdered. By controlling women and identifying certain types of intimate relations as immoral, the ownership and transmission of land and other forms of wealth could be regulated, class boundaries maintained and certain forms of labour, notably reproductive labour, obscured and appropriated. Colonial ideologies imposed hegemonic masculinity on the indigenous other, defining women and men as unequal opposites in a world structured by binaries. As we attempt to reconstruct past forms of kinship and marriage, it is crucial that we remember that, as a discipline, archaeology is profoundly interconnected with colonialism and its legacies.

Indigenous theorists have called into question Euro-American ideas about kinship, describing how in other cultural contexts kinship extends to non-human others, including plants and animals, sustained through relations of care, obligation and interdependency. In many indigenous communities, it is not sexual relations that determine rights over resources. Rather, it is relations with non-human others such as animals or the land itself that are central to the constitution of kinship. Abiding emotional attachments to place or links to totemic and ancestral animals define identity and ensure access to

Below: **In other cultural contexts, the boundary between people and animals is fluid and porous.**

resources. Indigenous ways of understanding the world indicate that trees or mountains or animals are not *like* kin but rather *are* kin. Western conceptions of kinship consider it possible for kin relations to exist only between humans. This is due to the distinctions that are drawn between culture and nature, self and other, and humans and animals; distinctions that serve particular ideological purposes in the present.

By stripping the non-human world of agency, western forms of kinship foreground and legitimize extractive rather than meaningful social relations between humans and non-human others. In contrast, indigenous scholars propose expansive definitions of kinship that encompass relations beyond those centred on procreation, ownership and control. These perspectives underscore the ties of mutual care and interdependency between humans and non-humans, which must be nurtured in order to ensure a sustainable world. They consider what it means to be 'in relation' with others and they propose an inclusive definition of kinship as the outcome of ongoing acts of mutual care. This perspective makes space for forms of kinship that are not predicated on sexual reproduction. It allows for alternative visions of gender and sexuality that can include other than humans as kin.

KINSHIP STUDIES

Set in this context then, it is little surprise that in fact Eurocentric formulations of kin and family are far from universal. Anthropologists have long discussed the extraordinary cross-cultural variability in the character and organization of kinship. There is always an element of cultural selection built into kinship systems. Some relationships are considered more significant than others. A study of kinship in southern India, for example (Busby 1997), has shown that the children of a woman and those of her brother are considered to be unrelated, as women pass on female substance to their children in the form of blood and breastmilk, while men pass on male substance in the form of semen. The children of a brother and sister, therefore, do not share the same substance. Genetic relatedness in other words does not directly translate to social relatedness.

This is because in many societies, although the physical process of procreation is acknowledged, it may not be considered socially significant. Evans-Pritchard's classic study of the Nuer people of South Sudan in the 1930s (Evans-Pritchard 1951) illustrated how cattle were said to beget children. Nuer fatherhood was not predicated on sexual relations with the mother but on the transfer of cattle in bridewealth transactions. If a woman's husband died, she could take a new partner but any children from the second relationship were considered to be the children of the man on whose behalf the bridewealth was originally paid.

In many other societies, too, biological parentage is not the primary determinant of kinship. Instead, kinship is viewed as socially and culturally constituted – as the outcome of social, not sexual, relations. Kinship is understood to be a product of social practices including ritual, exchange and the sharing of food. On the island of Langkawi in Malaysia, for example, kinship is viewed as an ongoing

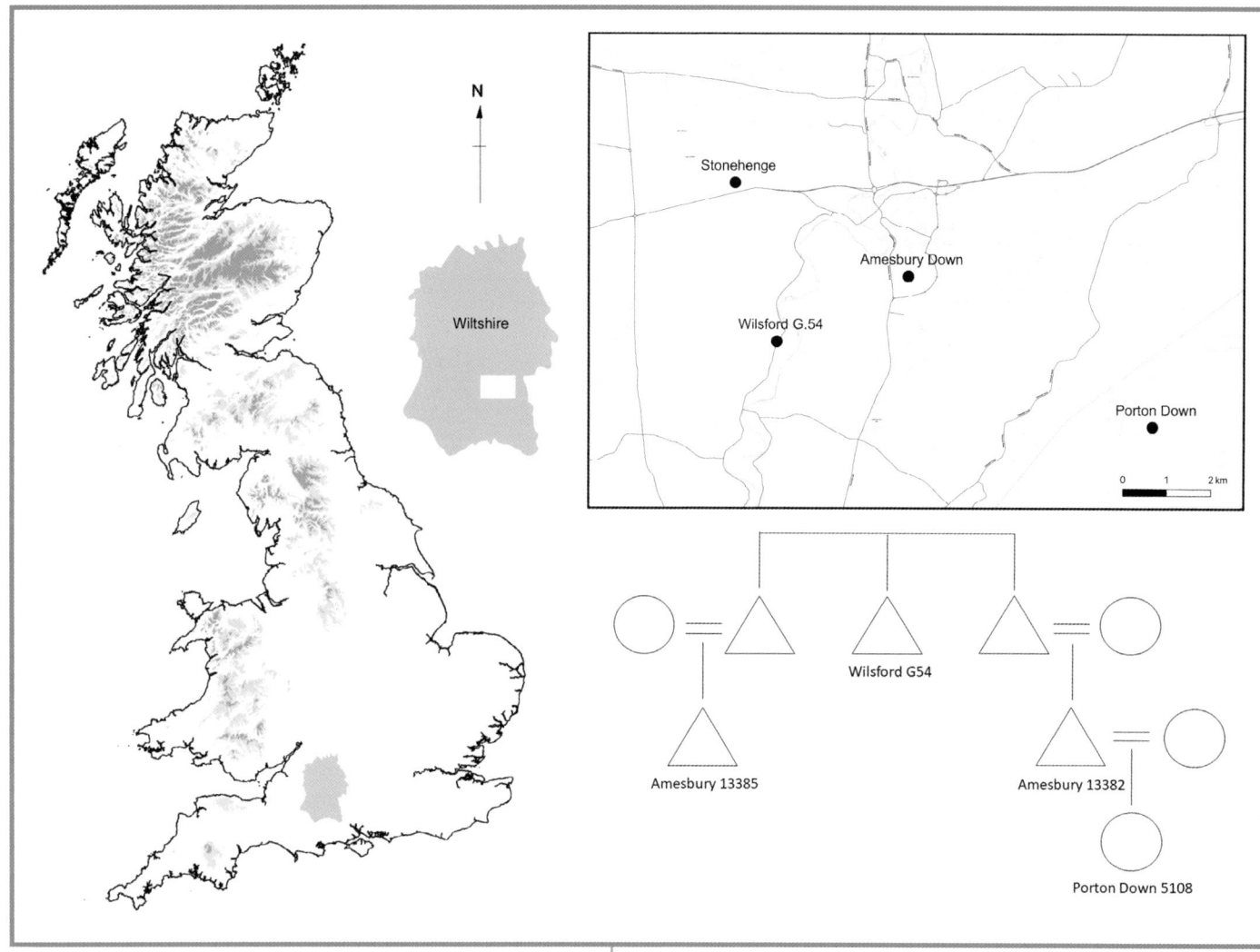

process that involves the sharing of substance (Carsten 1997). By living and eating together in the same house and by having children together, the blood of the husband and wife become increasingly similar over time. Foster children and other people related by marriage who eat food together also come to share the same blood.

Because kin are made, not determined by birth, kinship can be strategic and situational. In many parts of highland New Guinea, immigrants are quickly absorbed into local descent groups, as residence (and not genetic links) is the most important factor in deter-

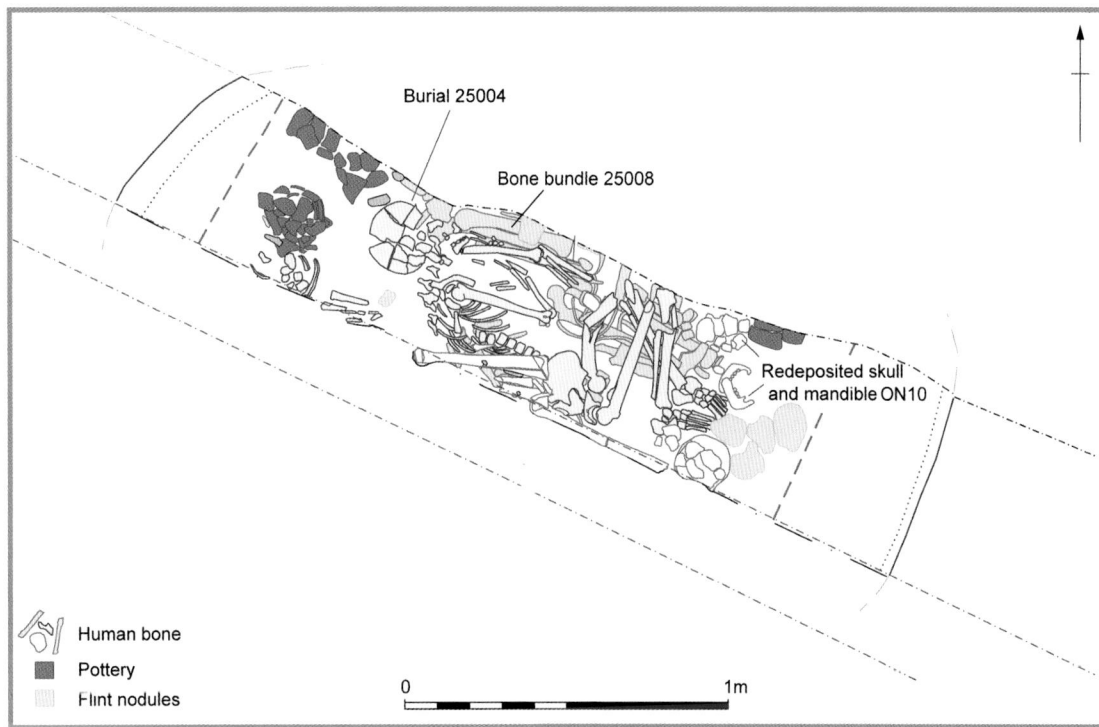

mining kinship. Although most societies in this region are patrilineal in principle (that is, they trace descent through the father's line) in practice, co-resident maternal kin and people related by marriage may be considered members of the descent group, while kin related through the paternal line who live at a distance may be forgotten.

Above: **(Fig 7) The Boscombe Bowmen, Wiltshire.**

Opposite page: **(Fig 6) Genetic relatives in the Stonehenge region. Circles represent females and triangles represent males.**

So, too, in many societies, different forms of kinship may be important in different contexts. In parts of Eastern Nigeria, for example, land is passed down through the paternal line but cattle, money and cult membership are inherited from maternal kin.

A final key point to draw from the anthropological literature on kinship before we turn to the archaeology is that although broad types of kinship organization can be identified, for example patrilineality, their sociopolitical implications and the way they operate in practice differ significantly from society to society. Gender ideologies and the position of women in patrilineal societies are

extremely variable, for example.

These observations have several significant implications for interpretation of the genetic evidence. Firstly, dominant Euro-American binary and heteronormative models of kinship and gender have their origins in a particular historical context and cannot be assumed to be universal. Secondly, genetic relationships are not the sole determinant of kinship. Rather, social practices of various sorts make kin, and kinship transcends biological links. The material world is often central to the creation of kin and non-human others can be considered to be kin. This suggests that there may be other ways of understanding how kin relations were constructed in the past that may be archaeologically accessible beyond the identification of biological links.

GENETICS AND KIN

Although aspects of the archaeology of Bronze Age Britain appear to fit the traditional narrative for the period of male-dominated societies, in fact, alternative readings of the mortuary data are also possible.

Here, I want to consider how to interpret the evidence for biological kinship presented in a recent study of archaeogenetic change in Early Bronze Age Britain (Olalde *et al.* 2018). Although the primary focus of that study was on genetic change at a population level rather than kinship, nonetheless genetic links were

---

Left: **Young man and woman from the same matrilineage buried together at Trumpington Meadows.**

identified between 16 individuals in their dataset. Twelve of these individuals indeed were related through the paternal line, suggesting that patrilineal descent was an important factor in the reckoning of social identity.

The most remarkable set of genetic relatives was a group of four individuals distributed across three cemeteries located within 10 kilometres of Stonehenge. Two adult men buried in neighbouring graves on Amesbury Down in Wiltshire were most likely paternal cousins (Figure 6). The daughter of one of these men was buried on Porton Down while their paternal uncle was buried on Wilsford Down, both just a few kilometres away (Booth *et al.* 2021). Another pair of paternal relatives from Amesbury Down was identified from the so-called Boscombe Bowmen grave (Figure 7). Here, the inhumation burial of an adult male was probably the paternal cousin or half-brother of an individual whose disarticulated skull had been placed at his feet. In this case, genetic relatedness is reflected in bodily and, presumably, social intimacy.

Anthropological studies of kinship demonstrate that even where there is patrilineal descent in principle, relationships with maternal kin continue to be highly important, facilitating access to land, goods, titles and so on. It is no surprise, therefore, that maternal relations were sometimes also foregrounded. The articulated burial of a 9–11 year-old female from Amesbury Down, for example, was placed in a pit adjacent to another pit containing an adult female skull and vertebrae. Ancient DNA and radiocarbon evidence suggest that the child was probably the genetic maternal aunt of the neighbouring burial. Although these individuals may never have met during life, their relationship was considered significant in death.

Elsewhere, a young man and woman buried together in the same grave at Trumpington Meadows in Cambridgeshire were second to third-degree relatives belonging to the same matrilineage. It is possible that matrilineal descent was the key principle of kinship organization in this community, hinting at regional variability in kinship structures. Radiocarbon dates on the remains of these two individuals are statistically indistinguishable. They may have been half-siblings related through their mother. In matrilineal societies, a woman's loyalty is to her brother, not her husband. Alternatively, they may have been the children of two sisters. Parallel cousins, that is, the children of same sex-siblings, are regarded as siblings in many societies and marriage between them is prohibited.

RESIDENTIAL MOBILITY

As previously noted, many scholars have suggested that women were exchanged as marriage partners by their male relatives in the Bronze Age. The argument that Bronze Age societies were patrilineal and practised virilocal marriage, where a woman moves to join her husband on marriage, is perhaps supported by the female burial from Porton Down discussed earlier. She was the genetic daughter of a man buried on Amesbury Down, some 6.5 kilometres to the north-west, so appears to have lived at a distance from her paternal kin (Figure 6). However, the reconstruction of residence patterns in this period is complicated by evidence for significant residential mobility. We cannot assume

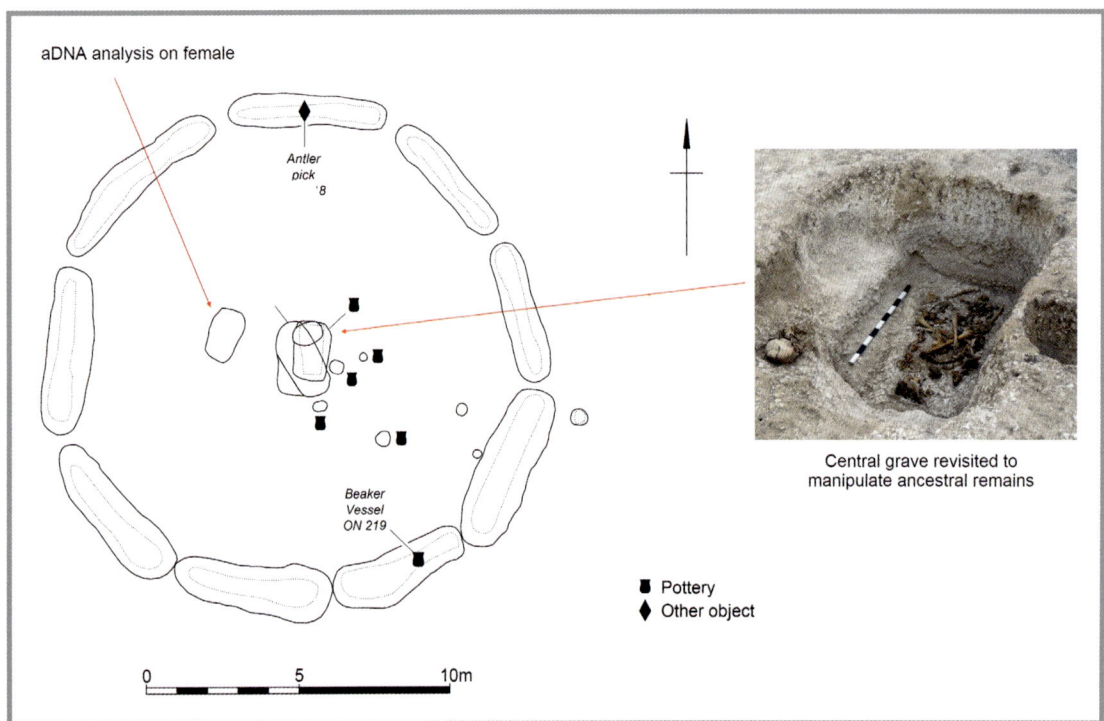

that relatives who are buried together actually lived together during life. Isotope analysis indicates that both men and women moved during this period and it is clearly problematic to assume that the movement of women was solely for the purpose of marriage when residential mobility, in fact, might have been a common life experience regardless of gender.

Certainly, Chalcolithic and Early Bronze Age cemeteries cannot be assumed to represent all members of a particular residential or kin group and other priorities may have determined place of burial. The woman from Porton Down, for example, was one of a group of burials of four females and six children in a segmented ring ditch (Figure 9). She lay approximately a metre to the north-west of a large grave at the centre of the monument that contained the disarticulated remains of another adult female. The central grave had been revisited to access and manipulate that

---

Above: **(Fig 9) Ring-ditch surrounding the graves of a number of women and children at Porton Down. The central grave had been accessed to manipulate the bones of a woman who may have been a person of significance.**

Opposite page: **The recut grave at Over, Cambridgeshire. Top: primary burial; bottom: later burial inserted into the same grave. Burials of genetically-unrelated individuals challenge us to imagine other forms of kinship.**

woman's bones. Her skull was missing, suggesting that it may have been retrieved for deliberate curation or re-deposition elsewhere. This female individual, therefore, may have been considered a significant ancestor and likely occupied a position of authority during life. The women buried in this monument were certainly not accorded social positions relative to men but rather on their own terms.

Cemeteries of this date in Britain are frequently interpreted as the burial grounds of particular descent groups because in many cases there is a linear element to the arrangement of graves that is thought to have reflected genealogical succession. However, ideas of kinship and descent may not have been wholly based on biological relatedness. At several sites, close spatial relationships between burials, which likely reflected intimate interpersonal ties in life, are not mirrored in the genetic data. At Windmill Fields, Ingleby Barwick in North Yorkshire, for example, four individuals were buried within a few metres of one another. Their radiocarbon dates suggest that they were broadly contemporary but none of them were genetic relatives. Here, co-residence may have determined kinship, as is common in many contemporary societies.

FORMS OF KINSHIP

I have already pointed out that the heteronormative character of kinship in the contemporary western world serves particular purposes, supporting a view of gender identity that is integral to colonial and capitalist modes of political and economic power. This

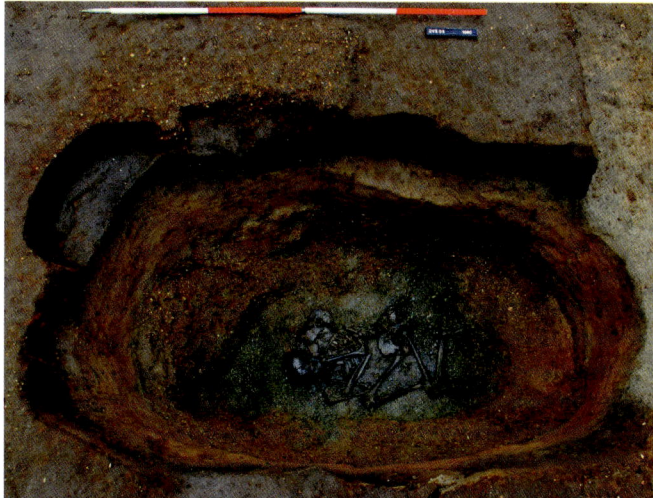

means that it is important to be open to exploring the archaeological evidence of other types of relationship.

At Over in Cambridgeshire, an adult female aged 18–25 years was laid at the base of a deep grave. The grave was subsequently recut and a second adult female more than 40 years old was interred. Their deaths were not many

Above: **(Fig 11) Objects were often deposited at significant places, suggesting social and emotional links with landscape.** *(Below)* **Middle Bronze Age pot found in a cleft in the rock at the Dewerstone, Devon** *(above).*

years apart but they were not genetically closely related. Anthropological studies of kinship suggests that there are various different ways in which this grave might be interpreted. It is possible that they were co-wives in a polygamous marriage. Alternatively, these burials might represent an instance of woman-to-woman marriage.

Historically, woman-to-woman marriage was widespread in Africa. A woman presumed to be barren could divorce her husband and remain in her father's home. She could then, herself, marry a woman whose children would count her as their father and who would be members of her patrilineage. Woman-to-woman marriage enhanced women's status and offered greater social and sexual freedom. It is also possible that the women from the Over grave were in an intimate same-sex relationship. This is something that is rarely considered in our discussions of kinship and marriage in the Bronze Age or indeed in general.

MAKING KINSHIP

Archaeogenetics clearly provides extraordinary new opportunities to understand kinship in the past. However, because of the valorization of science in contemporary academia there is some danger of prioritizing scientific data over other archaeological evidence for the making of kinship in the past. As archaeologists, we need to have more confidence in our ability to speak about different ways of relating.

Making kin involves material technologies. In the contemporary world, direct-to-consumer genetic testing kits do not so much reveal kin as make them, just as the material economies of love create and sustain ideologies of kinship in the present. Micaela di Leonardo, for example, shows how the task of making and maintaining kin relations is primarily assigned to women in contemporary North America and how the material world is central to that process, for example, by sending greeting cards and organizing holiday gatherings (di Leonardo 1987).

Archaeologists, of course, are particularly well-placed to investigate technologies of kinship in the past for these are directly reflected in material practice. In a Bronze Age context, as we have already described above, kinship is created in the spatial articulation and manipulation of the bodies of the dead. However, kinship was not solely located in the human body. The archaeological record also provides rich evidence for different technologies of kinship.

At Towthorpe in East Yorkshire, for example, a barrow covering the inhumation burial of an adult male was built of materials from three distinct sources: soil from the immediate vicinity of the barrow, clay from Burdale a mile to the west and clay from Dugdale a mile and a half to the north. The mound was composed of layers of these clays alternating with layers of soil from the immediate vicinity of the barrow and each kind of clay predominated at the side of the mound nearest the place from which it had been brought. Here, kin were made not through the bodies of the dead themselves but through other forms of social practice, in this case when people brought baskets of different materials from significant places in the landscape. In doing so, they marked the contribution of different kin groups to the substance of the deceased.

Archaeologists are well placed also to consider the implications of calls by indigenous scholars to move beyond models of kinship rooted in the heteronormative patriarchal and anthropocentric structures of settler sexuality. These scholars consider what it means to be in relation with others and they develop a more expansive and inclusive definition of kinship as the outcome of ongoing acts of mutual care. This perspective makes space for forms of kinship that are not predicated on sexual reproduction and that are open to including other than humans as kin.

Bob Johnston (Johnston 2021) has explored how kin relations in Bronze Age Britain were rooted in places invested with animate and ancestral powers. These relations can be traced in material interventions in the landscape such as the deposition of bronzes and other objects at striking landmarks. On Dartmoor in Devon, for example, a complete pot was found placed in a crevice, partway up the face of an imposing granite outcrop (Figure 11). This can be interpreted as an offering to ancestral spirits whose powers were vested in this place, a gesture of ongoing care towards ancestral lands and a manifestation of kin relations with both human and non-human persons.

Relations with animals may also speak of kinship links. Sometime, these were the intimate interconnections of everyday life. At Cliffs End Farm in Kent, for example, a sub-adult female lay flexed on her right side, her head resting on a cattle skull. It is possible that this animal had been gifted as part of the bridewealth of this young woman or her female kin (Figure 12).

Other relations may be more totemic in character. The cremation of a child at Skilmafilly in Aberdeenshire, for example, included a pair of burnt golden eagle talons. Totemic animals are usually understood as kin, the original progenitors of their human descendants. Their frequent slippage between human and non-human form in myth remind us that elsewhere the boundary between human and animal is not always viewed as categorically as it is in our own cultural context.

CONCLUSION

Bringing together theories of social practice with critical perspectives on the social significance of the biological links revealed by ancient DNA has much to tell us about kinship. Ancient DNA analysis has come to be viewed as the most accurate means of revealing prehistoric kinship structures. Yet, it is crucial that we avoid reading the genetic evidence in ways that unthinkingly impose contemporary conceptions of kinship and gender relations onto the past. A century of anthropological analysis of kinship and marriage demonstrates the extraordinary diversity of ways in which humans organize and understand their relationships with one another. We need to remain open to that diversity and consider alternative ways of

Above: **(Fig 12)** At Cliffs End Farm, a young woman was buried with her head resting on a cattle skull.

interpreting the archaeogenetic evidence that go beyond our own lived experience.

Moreover, kinship cannot be viewed as a direct reflection of genetic links. Kinship is not a given or 'natural fact' but is a process, the outcome of culturally prescribed social practices that require careful nurture, work and commitment. Archaeological evidence provides many insights into how relations were created and maintained through varied technologies of kinship, both focused on the body and beyond it. This is a different but complementary perspective to that offered by archaeogenetics, which identifies genetic links but does not immediately reveal their social significance. Most crucially though, we must move beyond biogenetic determinism to consider the ways in which social practice generated enduring affective bonds and the sharing of substance with both human and non-human others. These points have implications for our understanding of the Bronze Age more generally. They require us to question anthropocentric and androcentric notions of agency and to consider alternative concepts of gender, personhood and kinship.

Set within this context, it becomes easier to understand evidence that appears to challenge accepted models of Bronze Age society, such as the discovery of wealthy female burials, the decentralized production of high-status weaponry like swords, or the evident regional and contextual variability in how social identity was constructed.

Acknowledgements

I want to mark how much I appreciated Prof. Eogan's support as a student. I first met him in the late 1980s when I was still in school.

How well I remember those weeks [working on the Knowth excavations]. He took me along with some other Spanish and Austrian students to see archaeological sites right across the north-east of Ireland, bouncing about in the back of a UCD minibus.

He was less than impressed, though, when I tried to use one of the decorated stones from Knowth as a door prop in the tea hut! Thankfully, he forgave me and even invited me to stay with the Eogan clan one weekend when there were no other diggers around. I vividly remember a wonderful trip to his garden in Nobber to pick gooseberries.

BIBLIOGRAPHY

Booth, T., Brück, J., Brace, S. and Barnes, I. 2021. Tales from the supplementary information: ancestry change in Chalcolithic and Early Bronze Age Britain. *Cambridge Archaeological Journal* 31(2), 2021, pp1–22.

Busby, C. 1997. Of marriage and marriageability: gender and Dravidian kinship. *Journal of the Royal Anthropological Institute* (3), pp261–78.

di Leonardo, M. 1987. The female world of cards and holidays: women, families, and the work of kinship. *Signs* 12(3), pp440–53.

Evans-Pritchard, E. 1951. *Kinship and marriage among the Nuer*. Oxford: Oxford University Press.

Carsten, J. 1997. *The Heat of the Hearth: The process of kinship in a Malay fishing community*. Oxford: Oxford University Press.

Johnston, R. 2021. *Bronze Age Worlds: A Social Prehistory of Britain and Ireland*. Oxford. Routledge.

Olalde, I., Brace, S., Allentoft, M. *et al.* 2018. The Beaker phenomenon and the genomic transformation of northwest Europe. *Nature* (555), pp190–196 [Online]. Available from: https://doi.org/10.1038/nature25738 [Accessed 4 May 2023].

Chapter 4:

It is a great pleasure to honour George Eogan. We had a common interest in the Bronze Age and more specifically in Bronze Age metalwork and I have had cause to turn to his many fine publications on innumerable occasions.

DR STUART NEEDHAM

From Barrowscape to Fieldscape:
The First Fields in the Rother Region of the Western Weald

Dr Stuart Needham is former curator of the European Bronze Age at the British Museum and is now an independent researcher. In this paper he presents the results of the latest research into solstice alignments of fieldscapes and barrowscapes in the Rother Region of Hampshire and West Sussex, England.

The Rother Region lies on the edge of Wessex extending eastwards into what was in the past the supposedly dark forest of *Anderida*, otherwise known as the Weald. The Rother Valley is flanked by chalk uplands to the south and west and equally high sandstone uplands to the north. The Weald is a complex of varied sandstones, mudstones, siltstones and river-terrace mixtures, and even a little limestone. What has the Rother Region got to do with the Boyne Valley – surely this really is 'beyond' the Boyne? I can offer two connections.

The term 'The Bend of the Boyne' has

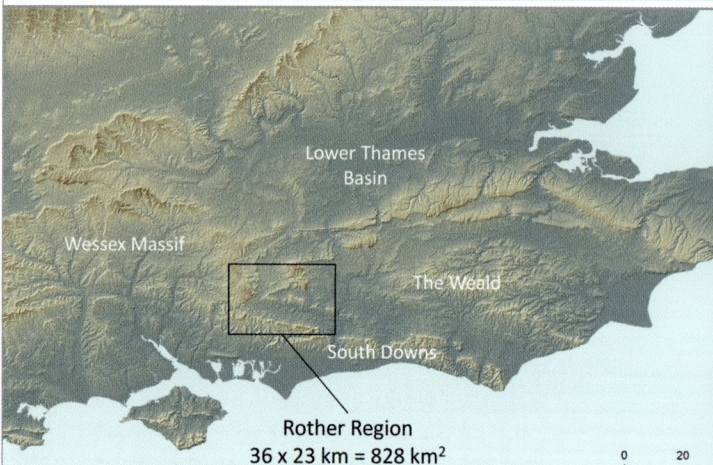

Above: **The Rother Region within the wider landscape of south-east England.**

Opposite page: **Barrows in the Rother Region; Petersfield Heath is located where the Rother changes course (arrowed).**

become common parlance in prehistoric archaeology but have you heard of 'The Bend of the Rother'? The western Rother River flows through the borderlands of Hampshire and Sussex but at Petersfield makes a very decisive change in direction from flowing south to flowing east. At this nodal point, on Petersfield Heath, lies the largest Early Bronze Age barrow group in the region. It comprised at least 28 barrows, most of them still surviving today.

The second connection is less prosaic: the observance and marking out of solstices, seen famously at Newgrange, turns out to be a recurrent feature of the Rother Region. Here we are dealing with a slightly later period, the Early Bronze Age, and a rather different set of manifestations, and both solstice axes appear to have been significant. Moreover, some of these alignments are embedded in the emerging fieldscape that succeeded the Early Bronze Age barrowscape.

BARROW DISTRIBUTION

The foundation for current research is the People of the Heath Project, now fully published (Needham and Anelay 2021a, 2021b, 2021c). Thanks to systematic scrutiny of LiDAR data and equally systematic ground-truthing, the number of recorded round barrows in the region has increased phenomenally (over 90 per cent) and now averages around one site per square kilometre, this despite the fact that they become sparse in the inner Wealden area. This fairly high density is within the typical range for the southern counties of England. There are a few limited areas with significantly higher

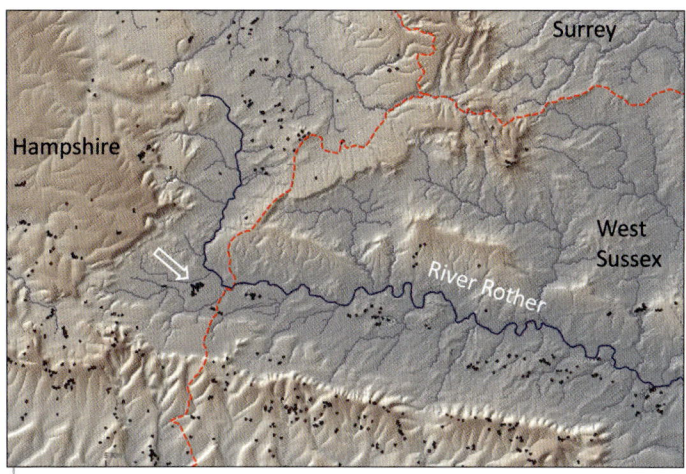

densities, notably the famous hotspots in western Wessex and the less well-known case of the Isle of Thanet in Kent. However, these special cases should be set aside when trying to interpret the more general pattern of barrows in southern England in terms of economy, demography and lifeways.

Much has been said and written about ritual and sacred landscapes in the Neolithic to Early Bronze Age. At times, areas dense in monuments have been seen as special set-aside reserves. In parallel, a further influential concept initiated by Andrew Fleming (Fleming 1971) linked uneven barrow density to transhumant societies. With the exception of special cases here and there, these models of land use and cosmography pose problems. Certainly, for the Rother Region the evidence is far more in favour of fairly small-scale and largely sedentary communities. The territories in Figure 4 have been deduced from the distribution of barrows (allowing for patterns of survival and destruction), patterns in their aggregation and topographic siting, and other contemporary evidence, which are all detailed in the People of the Heath publications (ibid.). Since stock keeping, especially of cattle, was probably a major part of the food economy, daily access to water was considered to be a vital factor in drawing the boundaries. The territories shown yellow on Figure 4 are distinguished by a high proportion of enclosure barrows and generally rather small mound barrows, so they have a distinct character. I have suggested tentatively that this zone may have been occupied by a quite different social group even, for example, at the ethnic level.

The sedentary model of settlement argued does not exclude a fair degree of personal mobility such as is now well attested by isotope studies (e.g., Parker Pearson *et al.* 2019) nor does it exclude internal seasonal or life-stage movement. This is well illustrated by the strontium isotope measurements for the buried individuals of Petersfield Heath. They were not all eating food from the same ecosystem, which may reflect diverse backgrounds from the varied geologies of the locality. Interestingly, none of the sampled

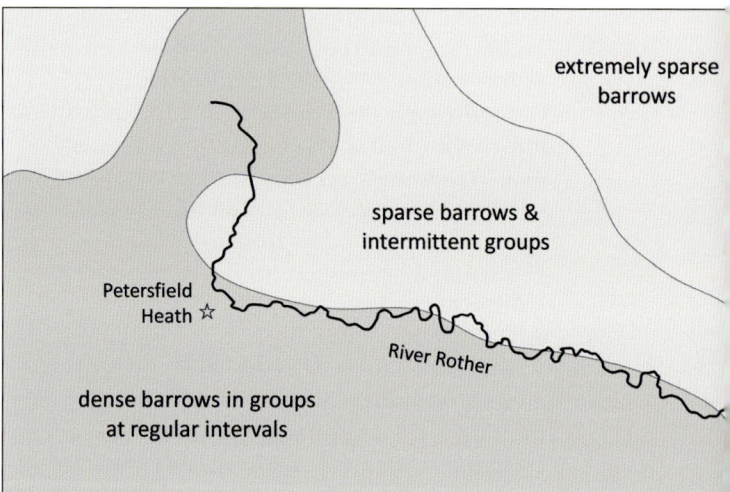

individuals seem to have been eating plants purely or predominantly from the nearby chalkland. There is also evidence for lifetime movement: the red arrow in Figure 5 links

Above: **Variations in barrow density in the Rother Region.**

Below: **(Fig 4) Territories of Early Bronze Age communities suggested for the Rother Region on the basis of round barrows and contemporary evidence.**

Opposite page: **(Fig 5) Strontium isotope analysis of people buried at Petersfield Heath suggests diverse backgrounds. On right, burial site of a possible female who had moved during her lifetime.**

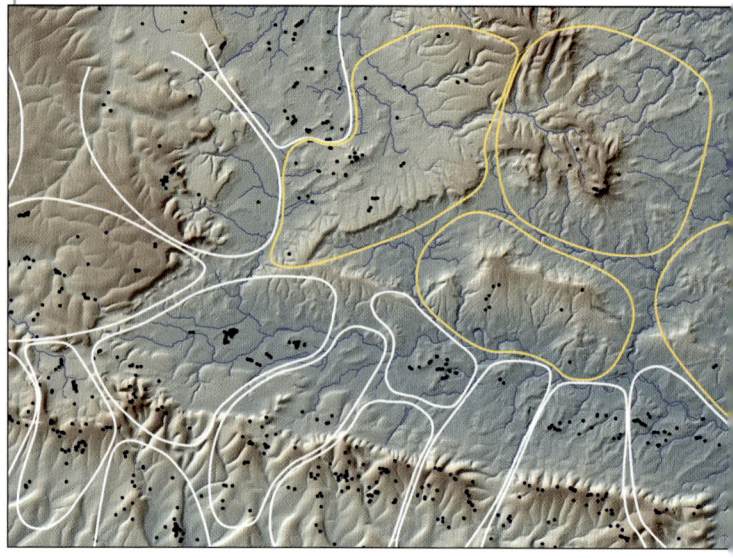

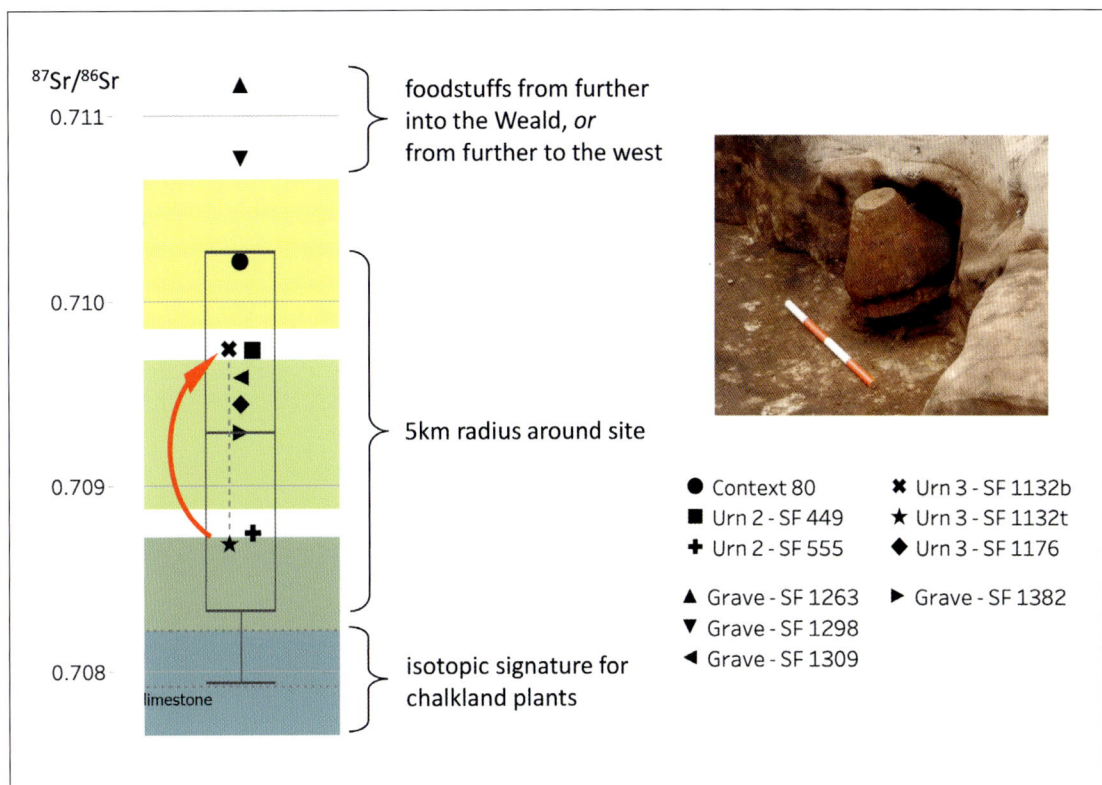

two samples from the same individual, a possible female from urn 3, barrow 19, who evidently had moved between childhood and young adulthood.

FIELD SYSTEMS

While it is now accepted that there was some chronological overlap between the construction of round barrows and field systems in southern Britain, it remains the case that it was very limited. The great majority of the barrows were constructed in the Early Bronze Age, before 1550 BC, while with rare exceptions the laying out of field systems did not precede the Middle Bronze Age. There has been much debate about the nature of this relatively swift transformation around the middle of the second millennium BC, whether it was grounded in economic, cultural or more cosmological concerns. A strong economic shift is evident, however, from the aggregated radiocarbon dates for carbonized plant remains collected by Stevens and Fuller (Stevens and Fuller 2012); it shows a strong upturn in cereals in southern and central England coinciding with the growth in field systems (Figure 6). Earlier, during the Neolithic and Chalcolithic, there appears to have been a significant exploitation of hazelnuts, perhaps a proxy for a heavy reliance on wild resources more generally. However, for the main barrow-building period, there are few dates for either of these plants and most food may have come from animals.

Barrows and fields give the impression of being two entirely separate phenomena. Barrows, usually clustered in groups, were for the burial of ancestral remains and other ritual purposes, while field systems were seemingly more concerned with food production and the necessities of everyday life. Yet barrow groups and field systems frequently occupy the same parts of the landscape. Barrows were respected in the sense that they were not obliterated when they lay within the fields. However, they ended up in varied positions in relation to the later imposed field boundaries – some at the boundaries, some in the middle of the fields, others somewhere in between. The fields appear to have been laid out according to their own independent rubric. Yet, it turns out that solstitial alignments provide some pivotal links between barrows and fields.

SOLSTITIAL ALIGNMENT

Starting with the barrow groups, solstitial alignments are particularly well illustrated by the main cemetery of Petersfield Heath. At midwinter, the sun sets in a prominent notch in the chalk ridge, the 'A3 notch', the line of view passing directly over the adjacent spring-fed marsh. The seven largest barrows, picked out in red in Figure 8, respect that alignment.

At the beginning of the same day, the sun

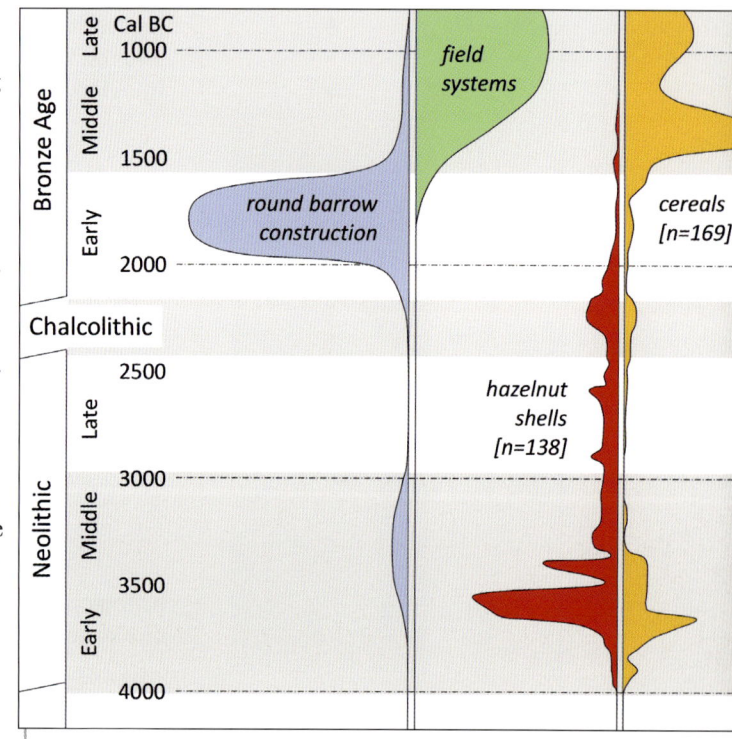

rises over a more distant notch in the same ridge. This notch is unremarkable in itself but it is exactly where lies the impressive Devil's Jumps – a barrow group in which the three largest barrows also are aligned on the north-west to south-east solstice. From The Jumps, the midwinter sun would be seen rising over the sea, trees permitting, and this event could be signalled to people down in the valley who would not see the sun rise over the chalk ridge for another few minutes. Thus is formed the 'solstice saltire' for Petersfield Heath incorporating The Devil's Jumps, the A3 notch, and also a barrow group at Broadway to the north-west. The north-east

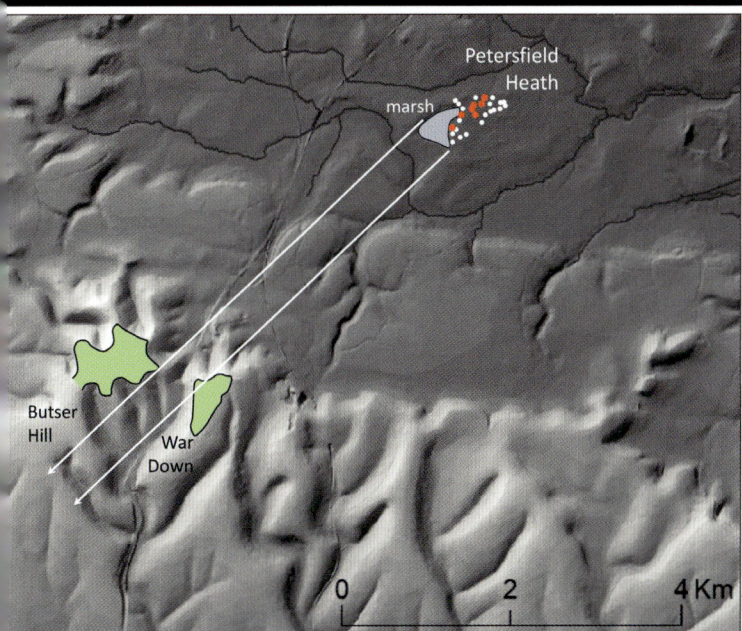

Above: The midwinter sun sets in the 'A3 notch' in the chalk ridge as viewed from Petersfield Heath.

Below: (Fig 8) The direction of midwinter sunset from the Petersfield Heath cemetery *c.*2000 BC (correction <1°). Barrows picked out in red are those with estimated volumes greater than 400m3. [volume fig 22.11 modified]

Opposite page: (Fig 6) Simplified time curves for round barrows, field systems, charred hazelnuts and charred cereals.

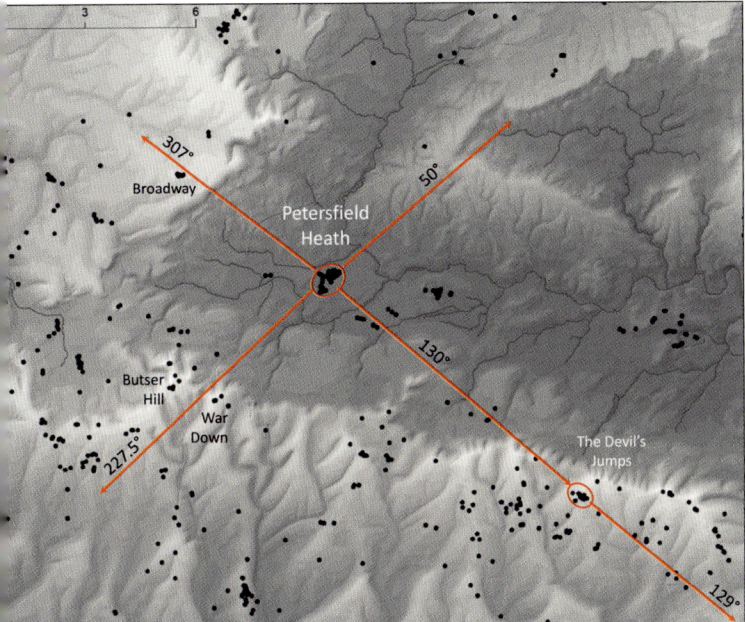

axis leads to the inner Weald where enclosure barrows are most frequent. As many as five examples occur on Petersfield Heath and suggest the cemetery may have had an inter-community bridging role.

These are not the only sites involved in solstice marking. Amongst a number of examples recognized, linear cemeteries at Heyshott Down and Woolmer Pond line up on the two different alignments although in the case of Heyshott Down only half of the cemetery is well aligned. It is worth noting that there are very few linear cemeteries like these in the Rother Region. The only other one that contains more than six barrows in linear formation is on Duncton Common. While this group does not in itself align on a solstice, one end falls on the north-west to south-east solstice line from an excavated ring ditch nearby, as does its central grave-like feature (Figure 11). The feature is surrounded by an arrow-like mortuary structure pointing north-west and open to the midwinter sun in the south-east. The presumed body within had decayed but three arrowheads and other flints were present. The barrow group on Sutton Common is somewhat different. The

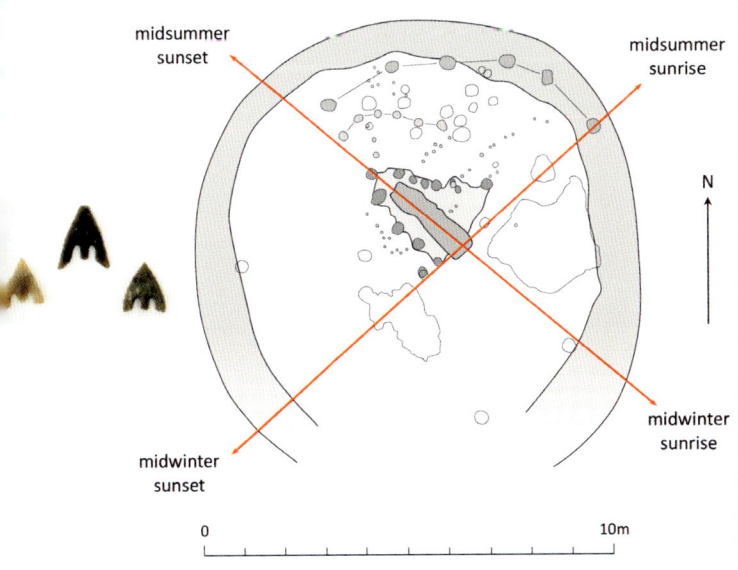

Above: **The 'solstice saltire' from Petersfield Heath cemetery. The alignments shown allow for the minor shifts since the Early Bronze Age and the inclination of observation lines.**

Left: **(Fig 11) Heath End, Duncton: interpretation of a ring-ditch showing solstitial structure, excavated by Casper Johnson, Archaeology South-East.**

Opposite page: **At The Devil's Jumps, Treyford Hill, the three largest barrows align on midwinter sunrise over the English Channel.**

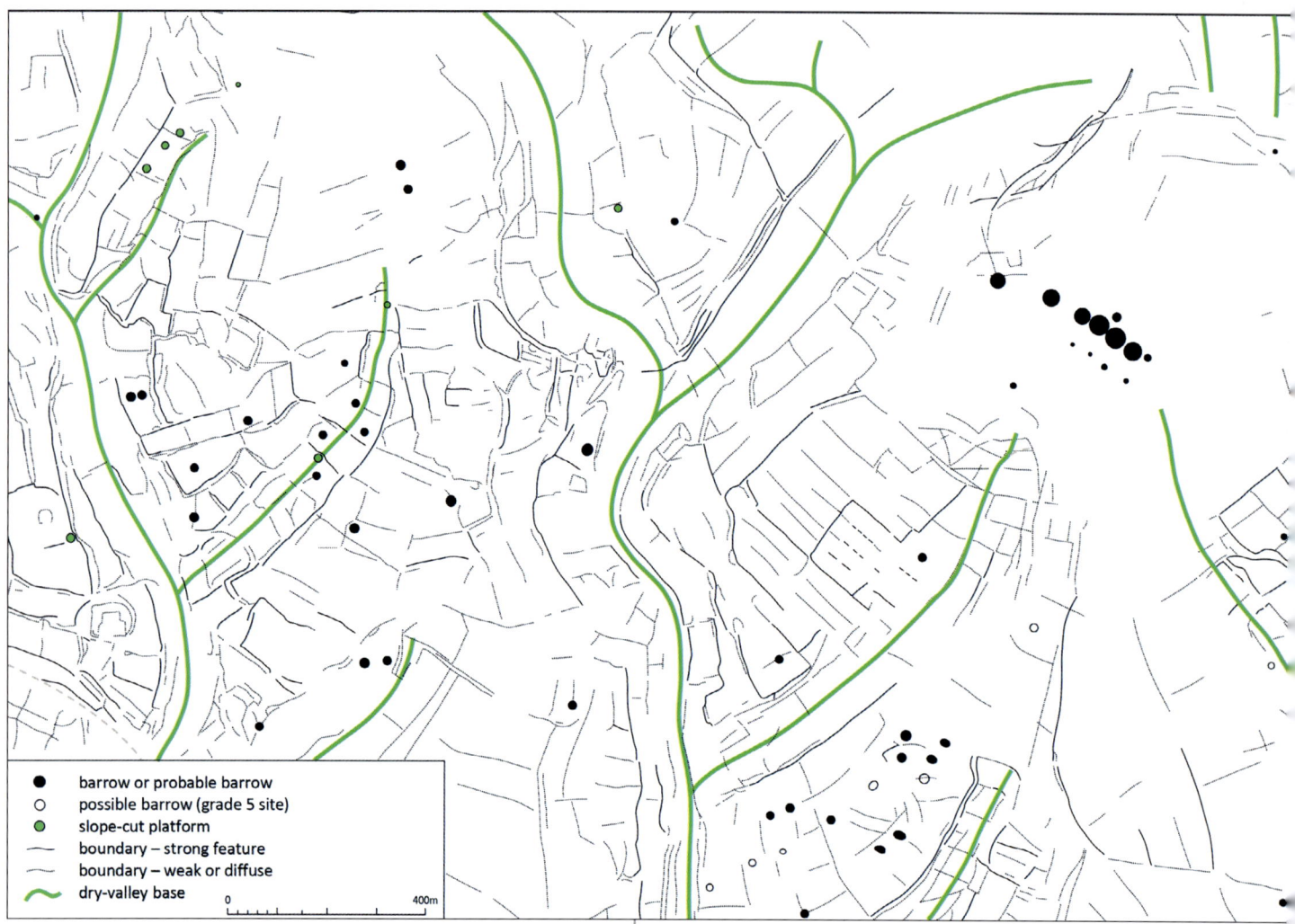

Opposite page: **(Fig 12)** Core block of fields overlying the circumferential barrow group of Linchball Wood. The green-shaded strips are suggested to be the founder-fields and are aligned on midwinter sunrise and midsummer sunset.

Above: **(Fig 13)** Barrows and field systems on the South Downs between North Marden Down and Treyford Hill. Possible house platforms are also shown.

barrows enclose a small dry valley that is aligned exactly on midwinter sunset and that line runs right through the largest barrow at the apex in the north-east.

So how are these cosmographical references amongst barrows relevant to the emergence of field systems? The currently documented ancient fields in this region are mainly on the chalk. They are only co-axial

over limited areas and often oriented perpendicularly to the local dry valley. It is also clear that they expanded piecemeal over time. Some almost certainly were being used and modified as late as Late Iron Age and Roman times when true ploughs were able to create substantial lynchets (cultivation-generated steps in the slope), which still survive today (Figure 15). So, there was undoubtedly a long history of evolution and reuse.

CONNECTIONS

At first sight it is hard to see much by way of a relationship between the barrowscapes and the overlying fieldscapes but detailed analysis reveals some key connections. At Linchball Wood, the barrow group is 'circumferential', in this case enclosing an area that included the confluence of three small dry valleys (Figure 12). Such dry valleys were likely traditional routeways up unto the high

chalk and thence down into the Rother Valley. In the environs of the cemetery the fields vary a lot in shape and orientation. There is, however, a more organized block of fields overlapping the barrow group and within this block are just two strips that are more consistent in plan than any others. One strip leads north-west from the largest barrow of the group, the other runs into the middle of the group. Both are aligned on midwinter sunrise to the south-east and on midsummer sunset to the north-west. Although subsequent field strips respect the same alignment in general, their layout quickly loses regularity. The implication is that the two regular strips were the first to be laid out.

An area a few kilometres to the west includes The Devil's Jumps already men-

Above: **(Fig 14) The core field blocks on North Marden Down** *(above left)* **and Philliswood Down** *(above right)***. The lighter grey tone is for fields suggested to have been next added.**

tioned, so, a solstitial alignment is known to have been marked out there already in the Early Bronze Age. Nearby are two other barrow groups at Phillis Wood and North Marden Down (Figure 13). The superimposed fields show a variety of patterns and, again, there is little sense of a single plan. However, in the midst of this rather incoherent pattern, there is a small block of regular rectangular field strips on Philliswood Down, lying between the three barrow groups (Figure 14). As in the case of Linchball Wood, regularity of layout and alignment on midwinter sunrise suggest this marks the beginning of field definition on this patch of downland. Whether this core block of fields was laid out in the Middle Bronze Age or, perhaps, towards the end of the Early Bronze Age does not alter the fact that the earliest fields evidently needed to encapsulate the critical solstice axis embedded in The Devil's Jumps just 400 metres to the north.

There is another possible early field block in this area that is of different character. It occupies a small dry valley, the lower half of which points instead to midwinter sunset. There is a possible house platform in a position to look down the valley towards this sunset. This south-west to north-east axis may have been anticipated in the barrowscape by the 'axial' barrow group of Phillis Wood, for this sits astride a solstice-aligned spur.

The Philliswood Down field axis may have been defined using barrows on spurs to the north-west and south-east. The barrows are 2.6 kilometres apart and would be intervisible if no trees stood in between. An observer on the north-west barrow near Telegraph House would be able to determine where this alignment crossed the intervening spur of Philliswood Down.

BARROW-FIELD PAIRING

Sabine Stevenson has identified other cases of small field blocks being aligned on midwinter sunrise in her PhD research (Stevenson 2023). In a fairly large area of the Heyshott and Graffham Downs, there is a block of fields with a predominant west-north-west to east-south-east alignment, thus not solstitial. However, amongst the few deviating alignments are two blocks with the north-west to south-east solstice alignment. One is a half kilometre south of the Heyshott Barrow group, which, as shown earlier, embodies the same alignment. This barrow–field pairing recalls the spatial relationship seen above for The Devil's Jumps and Philliswood Down.

Although prehistoric field systems are mainly seen on the chalk in the Rother Region, occasional examples are now being recognized on the sandstone uplands north of the river Rother, and at Goanah Farm near Petworth the solstice connection is repeated. Here a promontory drops west towards the Haslingbourne Stream. It has the most impressive barrow group on the Wealden side of the river, which was succeeded by a field system that was cultivated long enough to produce large lynchets on some boundaries. The system is not very regimented, boundaries being partly dictated by topography (Figure 15). Nevertheless, the core axis does not follow the axis of the promontory but instead points to midwinter sunset. By coincidence or choice, the small valley along-

side points in the same direction. It has permanent running water and there are probable prehistoric house platforms still visible in the ground today to either side.

So, various solstitial alignments have been recognized in a small region both in barrow groups and in core field blocks. The recognition of intended solstitial alignments in prehistoric monuments no longer comes as a surprise and, as others have argued, this is not self-explanatory in terms of particular beliefs or objectives. They are the special cases that correspond to the limiting standstills of the sun, hence we can have a high degree of confidence in their intentionality. Other orientations in between also may have been significant to the barrow- or field-constructing communities but are less capable of independent validation. It is noteworthy, for example, that 17 of 20 linear elements (four or more barrows in a line) in the region have alignments spread through the solar arc rather than being focused on the two limits.

Two things stand out from the evidence for alignments in the Rother Region. One is the goodly number of them, such that we are beginning to see a lattice formed by the two solstice axes criss-crossing much of the region, a lattice that embraces prominent natural features as well as the made earthworks. The second is that the alignment evidence has allowed us to make for the first time a substantive connection between two utterly different earthwork categories.

ANCESTRAL CONNECTIONS

Despite the radical difference between barrowscapes and fieldscapes in terms of mor-

Above: **(Fig 15) Goanah promontory, near Petworth, from the west showing some of the prominent lynchets.**

phology, layout principles and primary purpose, there are important aspects of continuity in this regional landscape. Frequently, there is a connection between an important barrow group and an early block of fields. Perhaps we can go a bit further and suggest that the core field blocks are actually contemporary with the main round barrow era and that these provided the obvious springboard from which the extensive field systems developed from the Middle Bronze Age onwards.

This potential early dating has all sorts of implications. As we have seen, the wider evidence suggests a direct relationship between the growth of field systems and increasing cereal production, so the positioning of the initial field blocks could suggest the need for the ancestral protection of cereal growing plots. Moreover, they were given a very specific alignment that explicitly embedded the turning point of the annual cycle. In the process of expansion over time these primary principles seem to have dissipated or were modified.

Even before the early field blocks were delineated on the ground, I suggest that the areas that are dense in barrows, whether on the uplands or on lower heathlands, were well utilized parts of the landscape and not just marginal reserves for the dead. In *Barrows at the Core of Bronze Age Communities*, it is suggested that an overarching role of barrows was that they provided ancestral guardianship of the land in which they oversaw a range of critical resources – economic to spiritual – being concerned with the control of land, raw materials, communication routes and places deemed to be sacred. Barrow grounds played a critical part in the occupation of the land in its fullest sense and can be seen as ancestral to the age of fieldscapes, despite their entirely different character.

BIBLIOGRAPHY

Fleming, A. 1971. Territorial patterns in Bronze Age Wessex. *Proceedings of the Prehistoric Society* 37, pp138–66.

Needham, S. and Anelay, G. 2021a. People of the Heath Project. [Online]. Available from: http://www.peopleoftheheath.com/publications/ [Accessed 25 April 2023].

Needham, S. and Anelay, G. 2021b. *Barrows at the Core of Bronze Age Communities: Petersfield Heath excavations 2014–18 in their regional context*. UK. Sidestone Press.

Needham, S. and Anelay, G. 2021c. *Barrows at the Core of Bronze Age Communities: Supplementary Material*. UK. Sidestone Press.

Parker Pearson, M., Sheridan, A., Jay, M., Chamberlain, A., Richards, M.P. and Evans, J. (eds) 2019. *The Beaker People: Isotopes, Mobility and Diet in Prehistoric Britain*, Prehistoric Society Research Paper 7. Oxford: Oxbow.

Schulting, R., Pouncett, J. and Snoeck, C. 2021. Strontium isotopes on cremated human remains *IN*: Needham, S. and Anelay, G. 2021b, pp275-81.

Stevens, C. and Fuller, D. 2012. Did Neolithic farming fail? The case for a Bronze Age agricultural revolution in the British Isles. *Antiquity* 86, pp707–22.

Stevenson, S. 2023. Cosmology in the Rother valley landscape of the Western Weald: Bronze Age metalwork deposition and field systems under rising mist and setting Sun. Unpublished University of Winchester PhD thesis.

Chapter 5:

One of George Eogan's main interests was megalithic art. Through his excavations at Knowth from 1962 onwards, he was involved in uncovering the biggest collection of megalithic art at any one site either in Ireland or beyond.

DR ELIZABETH SHEE TWOHIG

Megalithic Art in the Boyne Valley and Beyond

Dr Elizabeth Shee Twohig is a former Senior Lecturer in the Department of Archaeology, University College Cork, and a leading expert on megalithic and rock art in Ireland and Western Europe. She prepared the results of George Eogan's work on the megalithic art at Knowth for publication in 2022 by the Royal Irish Academy. In this paper, she presents a summary of the various styles of megalithic art identified at Knowth and compares these with other megalithic art in the Boyne Valley and elsewhere in Ireland and beyond.

There are three main passage tombs with megalithic art in the Boyne Valley (Knowth, Dowth and Newgrange) as well as the middle-sized cairn that was discovered at Dowth Hall in 2017 (Figure 2). These sites were built and had their initial period of use in the period

Left: Newgrange and nearby passage tombs, looking east.

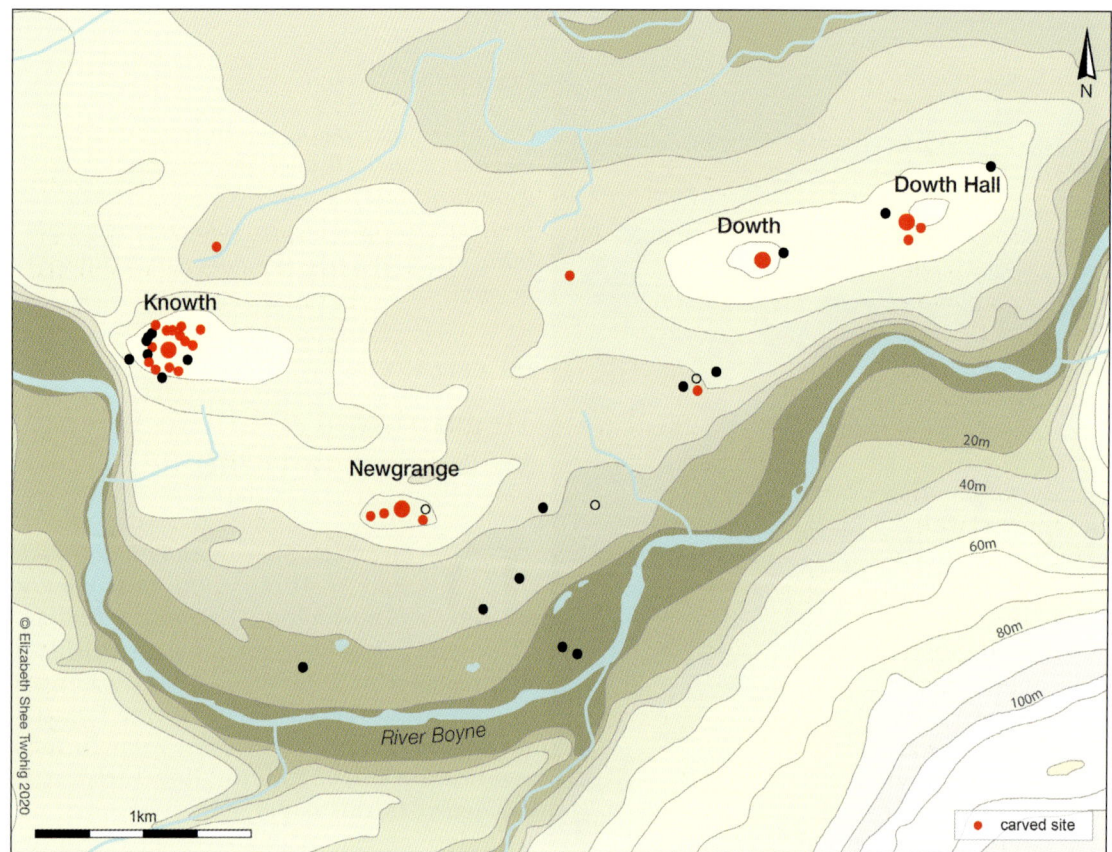

3200–2900 BC. Some other examples of art also occur in the area, including in smaller tombs surrounding or adjacent to larger ones as well as a few examples of single stones, perhaps the last remnants of destroyed passage tombs.

Above: **(Fig 2) Map of the Boyne Valley passage tombs and possible passage tombs, showing carved sites in red.**

Opposite page: **(Fig 3) Numbers of carved stones at Irish passage tombs and passage tomb-style stones.**

Megalithic art has been known at Newgrange since the site was first reported in 1699 and many new examples were found during excavations between 1962 and 1975 by the excavator, M.J. O'Kelly. These were published in collaboration with Claire O'Kelly, who had main responsibility for recording the art at Newgrange. She made the drawings and wrote the catalogue of the carved stones there, which was published in her own book (C. O'Kelly 1978) and also in the excavation report (M.J. O'Kelly 1982) in which she contributed the chapter on the carvings.

Excavations carried out at Knowth by R.A.S Macalister in 1941 uncovered some carvings on the kerbstones of the main tomb (Knowth 1) and in one adjacent small tomb, Tomb 14 (Eogan and Cleary 2017, p17–18). George Eogan's excavations revealed almost 350 additional stones with carvings, particularly in the two large tombs of Knowth 1, which were found in 1967 and 1968, and these are now fully published (Eogan and Shee Twohig 2022; see therein for further details). In Ireland as a whole, the numbers of carved stones that have been recorded show that the Boyne Valley, and in particular Knowth 1, dominates with $c.$46 per cent of the carvings (Figure 3). However, the recent recognition of extensive area-picking on stones at Newgrange means that these statistics need to be revised to factor in $c.$50 additional carved stones at Newgrange (see below).

Passage tombs with art are distributed from Antrim southwards to Knockroe, County Kilkenny (Shee Twohig and Cleary 2022, fig. 1.1). At Knockroe, excavations revealed 35 decorated stones (Muiris O'Sullivan pers. comm.); these include a number of examples that are comparable in quality with those in the Boyne Valley, notably in the western tomb. Further similarities between Knockroe and the Boyne Valley sites include the fact that the two tombs at Knockroe are aligned on mid-winter (solstice) sunset and sunrise (O'Sullivan 2004).

The other main site with carvings is the passage tomb cluster at Loughcrew, County Meath, where a series of passage tombs on three hilltops have carvings, particularly those on the central and western hills (Shee Twohig 1981, p203–220). In Figure 4, the photograph shows some of the carvings in Cairn T, which is the dominant cairn on the central hill. Cairn T is the highest cairn of the group and its passage is aligned on sunrise at the spring and autumn equinoxes. It is noteworthy that the carvings on the stones along the main axis of the structure have sun-like radial pattern motifs.

The distribution map of Irish megalithic art (Shee Twohig and Cleary 2022, fig. 1.1) became out-dated in August 2022 when archaeological photographer Ken Williams found a stone with very clear carving forming part of one of the best-known archaeological sites in the country, the large stone circle at Grange, Lough Gur in County Limerick. The carving is on the back of one of the stones of the circle. There is probably more carving lower down because the back of the stone is partially hidden by the bank that encircles the stone circle, and the carving

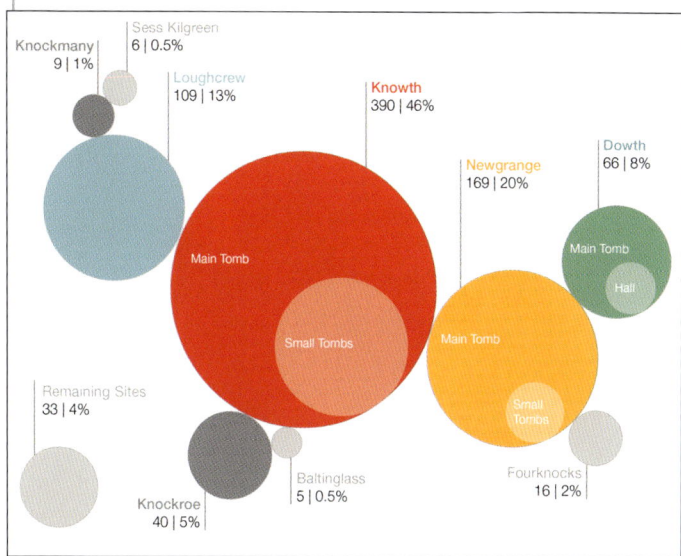

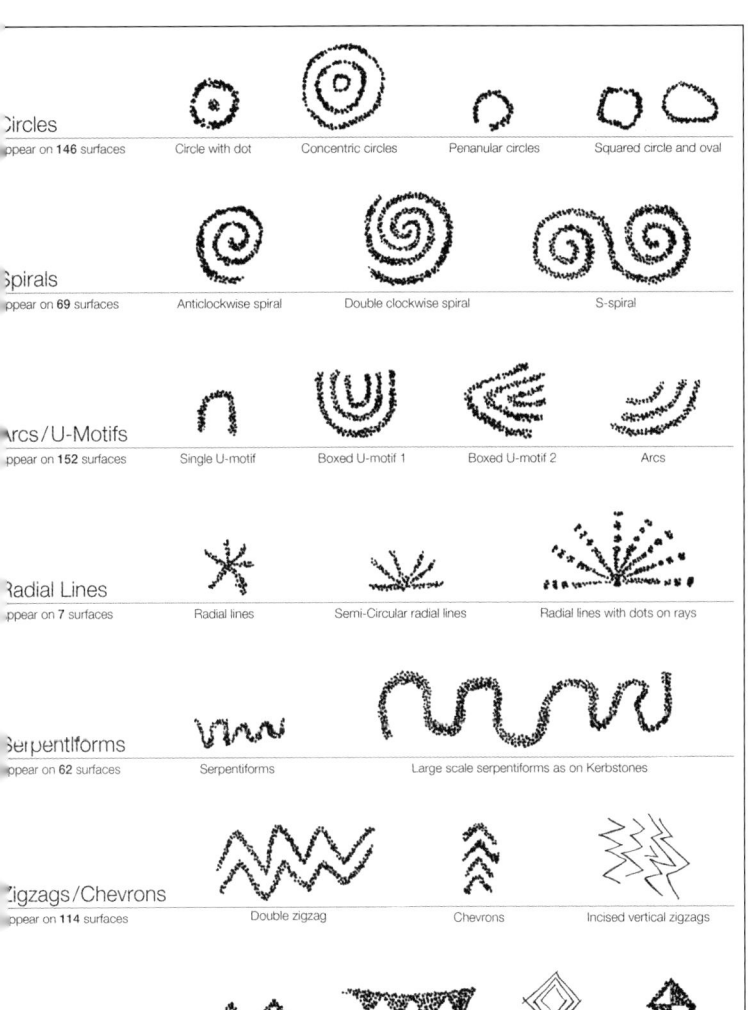

ART STYLES

Besides almost doubling the number of known examples of megalithic art in Ireland, the two well-preserved tombs in Knowth 1 provided the opportunity to investigate the details of the carvings and the finer incised designs and yielded much important new information about how the carvings were made. In contrast, the small tombs around Knowth 1 had been damaged in various ways and the stones were much more weathered, with many missing by the time the tombs were excavated. Examining the different styles of art that we have identified at Knowth and in other locations of passage tomb art makes a useful framework for talking about megalithic art generally. It has been possible to identify seven styles of art in Ireland, with Standard Megalithic Art found most extensively. Knowth has the greatest range of styles, followed by Newgrange, whereas most other sites show only occasional divergences from the Standard Megalithic Art style. At Knowth it has been possible to determine the sequence of carvings to a certain extent, which is a subject that George Eogan published on over the years in papers, and spoke about at conferences.

What I call 'Standard Megalithic Art' is the kind of art that is found throughout the Boyne Valley and also in the rest of Ireland. Within this style there is a variety of motifs and a also comes around the sides of the stone. The style of carving here is very close to that at Knockroe, to the east (Williams 2023).

Above: **(Fig 5) Diagram showing the principal motifs of Standard Megalithic Art in Ireland.**

Opposite page: **(Fig 4) Cairn T interior, Loughcrew, County Meath, looking towards the backstone with sillstones in the foreground.**

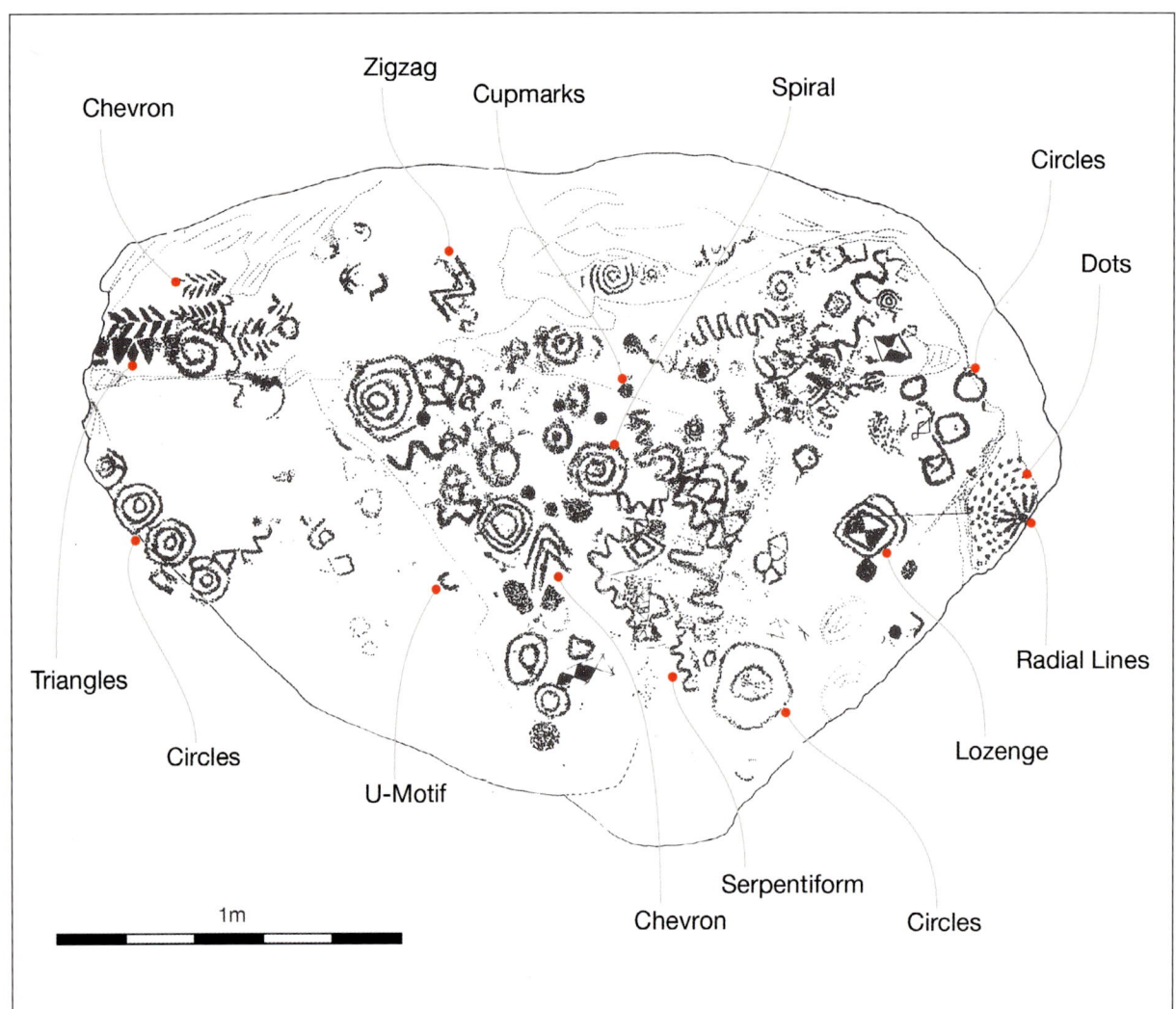

Above: **(Fig 6) The principal motifs in Standard Megalithic Art, recorded on Orthostat 8b, Tomb 14, Knowth.**

Opposite page: **(Fig 7) Orthostat 81 in Tomb 1 West, Knowth, with Recycled Style Art.**

range of carving techniques. Picked line motifs are most common, but finely cut or incised lines can also be found, especially when a stone is well preserved. Sometimes incised lines are used in their own right but sometimes the incised line provides an outline for other motifs, particularly for a kind of panel of carving where picked areas alternate with unpicked ones, creating a kind of checkerboard effect, usually of lozenges or triangles.

A diagram (Figure 5) of the main range of the motifs shows circles of different kinds and shapes such as irregular ovals and circles with squared corners; spirals of different kinds, sometimes single, or a double spiral (where one is inside the other) or, occasionally, S-spirals; arcs of various kinds; radial line motifs like those noted at Loughcrew Cairn T; serpentiforms; zigzags; lozenges and triangles and a combination of the two where a lozenge is subdivided into triangles with area picking.

One particular stone, orthostat 8 in Tomb 14 at Knowth (Figure 6) shows all of these on a single surface as well as a number of cup-marks. Often cupmarks are found in what appear to be interesting places, often on significant points of a kerbstone, perhaps marking something of importance.

RECYCLED ART

The next art group I want to discuss is a very unusual type of art that uses almost exclusively only two of the Standard Megalithic Art motifs, the spiral and the zigzag. The spirals are very finely carved with their circuits set closely together, and the segments of the zigzags tend to be slightly curved. The picked lines are often slightly rubbed. This style is what George Eogan called Recycled Art and there are 21 definite examples at Knowth (Shee Twohig 2022b). He argued that stones with carvings in this style were built into the tombs, perhaps having already been used at some other monument, which he tentatively named 'Tomb 1A'.

This Recycled Art is mainly found in the two big tombs of Knowth 1, in the inner section of the eastern tomb and in the outer section of the western tomb. A corbel very high up in the roof of Knowth 1 East tomb is a good example, where one can see how much of the carving is hidden where it runs in behind the other corbels that support it (Shee

Twohig 2022b, fig. 4.4). The carving was clearly done before the corbel was put in place and shows that this style of carving is earlier than or contemporary with the building of the big tombs. The same applies to most of these Recycled Art stones. In two examples in the passage of Knowth 1 West, the carving extends over most of the surface of the stones but, when they were reused in the extension of the western tomb, a large section of the carved area was hidden by being buried in the socket (Figure 7). This was found when the stones and others in this passage were excavated and taken out prior to the modern reconstruction of that section of the tomb.

There are a few other examples of the Recycled Art style in the Boyne Valley, most notably on the well-known stone labelled L19 in the passage at Newgrange. While it is a well-known stone, it is difficult to photograph because it is very close to the stone opposite it in the passage. The photograph in Figure 8 was created by 'stitching' together several photographs to produce a very fine full-on image. There again the spirals and the zigzags can be seen but lower down there is another set of spirals and zigzags that are almost obscured by pick dressing over the whole surface as was done at the very top of the stone. This picking leaves the main panel of spirals and zigzags standing out slightly from the rest of the stone's surface.

Another example of such Recycled Art at Newgrange is known from an early drawing of a corbel near the end chamber at Newgrange, which also had spirals and zigzags (Shee Twohig 2022b, fig. 4.8). This corbel cannot be seen now, because there has been a shift in the stones at that point.

There are a few other examples of carvings similar to Recycled Art but their locations are widely dispersed. I include with these Orthostat 5 in Cairn B, in Carrowkeel, County Sligo, which has zigzags and spirals at the top (Hensey and Robin 2011) and a carved stone from Clear Island, County Cork (Shee Twohig 2022b, plate 4:8). Another example can be seen at Barclodiad y Gawres in Anglesey, Wales, a tomb that really is part of the Irish passage tomb group. One stone there has a weathered spiral at the top right as well as zigzags that can be seen more clearly (Figure 9). Where this style of art developed is difficult to understand but it clearly belongs to an early stage of Irish megalithic art.

LARGE SCALE KERBSTONE ART

Another style of carving that is more or less exclusive to Knowth is what I have called 'Large-scale Kerbstone Art'. Many of the kerbstones there (and at Newgrange) are over two metres across and at Knowth they are often carved with just a single very large motif, usually a circle with arcs, or serpentiforms. Sometimes, the large carving overlies finer carving underneath, as one can see on Kerbstone 47 where on the top left there is a small, finely picked spiral that is overlain by the big motif that occupies most of the stone (Figure 10). Although this kind of art is

Above: **(Fig 9)** Orthostat C16 at Barclodiad y Gawres, Anglesey, Wales.

Opposite page: **(Fig 8)** Orthostat L19 in the passage of Newgrange with Recycled Style Art and area picking.

mainly a feature of Knowth, Kerbstone 67 at Newgrange (Figure 11) is rather similar with a large S-spiral design and some much smaller carvings, which are probably earlier.

RIBBON-LINE ART

The other style that is very distinctive and is found almost exclusively at Knowth is the Ribbon-line Art that occurs within the inner

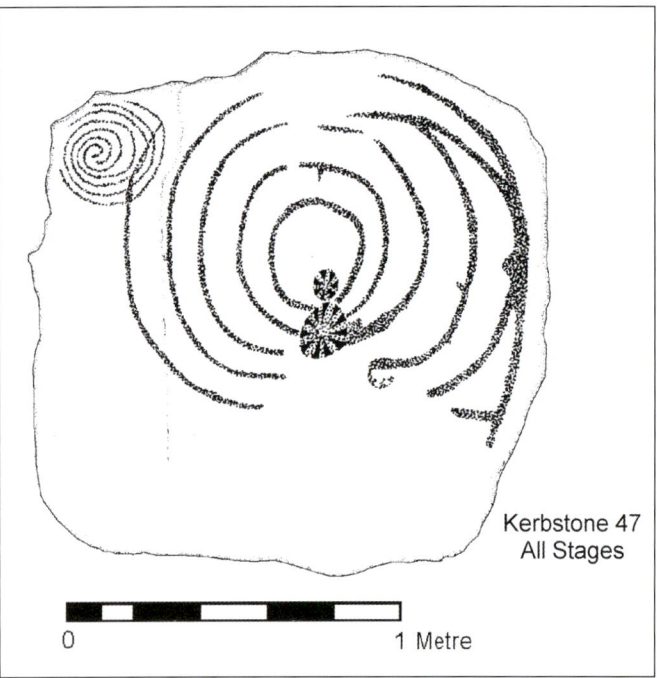

Kerbstone 47
All Stages

0   1 Metre

section of the two tombs in Knowth 1 but rarely elsewhere, and then in a slightly different form. It does not use many motifs, mostly just simple circles and arcs, but they are deployed in an unusual way in that the carving covers the whole surface of the stone in swirls. It seems almost as if it is creating a presence to guard the tomb (Figure 12). Several examples occur near the entrance area to the inner section of the tombs (Shee Twohig 2022b, figs 4.12 and 4.13). The kerbstones at the entrances to both passage tombs feature a similar design,

Above: **(Fig 10) Knowth Kerbstone 47, showing Large-scale Kerbstone Art style overlying an earlier spiral.**

Right: **(Fig 11) Newgrange Kerbstone 67.**

but in a more rectilinear form (Figure 13). Several of these stones also feature small, earlier motifs underneath the main Ribbon-line art.

The art on the remarkable basin stone in the eastern tomb of Knowth 1 also belongs to this style, with ribbon lines around the sides and also inside the basin (Shee Twohig 2022b, plate 4:20). There are possibly two phases displayed here. The carving on the front, facing into the chamber, has simpler crescents and circles and narrower lines and the carvings in the central area inside the basin are similar (Figure 14). What is also interesting is that four vertical lines are carved on the side of the basin, in a pattern that recalls pottery found in Brittany. This pottery occurs in a particular type of monument called an angled-passage tomb, which belongs in the later stages of passage tomb construction in Brittany and is contemporary with the big Irish passage tombs. In those angled-passage tombs there also are carvings that are quite like the Ribbon-line Art at Knowth.

The Ribbon-line art also appears on a 300mm long phalliform stone that was found outside the western tomb; it bears ribbon-like grooves along its length, with circles and crescents around the wider end (Shee Twohig 2022b, fig. 4.18). Limestone pieces of the same shape and with almost identical designs are known in southern Portugal in the Alentejo/Tagus estuary area; there are also plain ones, including an example of similar size found at Newgrange (O'Kelly 1982, fig. 56).

As already noted, a version of Ribbon-line Art is used on the kerbstones at the entrances to both the eastern and western tombs at Knowth where the Ribbon-line art is deployed

in a rectangular style (see Figure 13). A vertical line marks the centre of both these stones, signalling the location of the entrance to the passage. Similar vertical lines also occur at Newgrange, on the entrance stone and on Kerbstone 52 at the rear of the tomb, though on Kerbstone 52 the vertical line is shown as a quite broad band (Shee Twohig 2022c, plates 5:4 and 5:5). A shallow vertical band is also carved on the back of the kerbstone at the entrance to the tomb of Dowth South (Shee Twohig 2022a, plate 3:28).

PICKING

Picking is a type of carving that occurs quite extensively at Knowth and both George Eogan and Muiris O'Sullivan have argued that this is a form of art. One style is best described as Dispersed Picking, where the pickmarks are placed at a distance from one another. This form is found most extensively in the inner part of the western tomb at Knowth, occurring on the corbels, the orthostats and even on the underside of the roof stones (Figure 15). The

Above: **(Fig 13) Kerbstone 74, Knowth Tomb 1, at the entrance to the western tomb**

Right: **(Fig 14) Basin stone in Knowth Tomb 1 East.**

Opposite page: **(Fig 12) Orthostat 69 Knowth Tomb 1 East, showing Ribbon-line art.**

other style of picking that is often found at Knowth is where the pickmarks are set close together and we have called that Amorphous Close Area-picking – amorphous because it mostly does not form any shape, and close because it is not dispersed or spread out, as in Dispersed Picking (Figure 16).

Picking is also found at Newgrange, and it occurs to a much greater extent than has been noted hitherto. Ken Williams and I were fortunate to be granted some funding to work within Newgrange during the period when visitors were not allowed inside the monument due to Covid 19 restrictions. We spent several days inside the tomb in 2021, to carry out a written and photographic inventory of the carvings. Inside the tomb, the O'Kellys had noted the presence of picking but had not documented it in detail, a task that in any case would have been almost impossible with the camera and lighting equipment available in the 1960s and 1970s, as well as the difficulties in examining the upper part of the

Above: **(Fig 15) Dispersed picking in the inner section of Knowth Tomb 1 West.**

Opposite page: **(Fig 16) Tomb 1 East Orthostat 46, showing Amorphous Close Area-picking.**

corbelled roof, where the capstone at the top is six metres above ground level.

Looking upwards into the corbelled roof of the chamber at Newgrange, the bottom face of the capstone can be seen (Figure 17). This recent photograph shows the Close Area-picking on the corbel stones, which must have been done when the stones were in place as the aim was clearly to knock off any protru-

Opposite page, above: **(Fig 17) Amorphous Close-area Picking on corbels supporting the chamber capstone at Newgrange.**

Opposite page, below: **(Fig 18) Amorphous Close-area Picking on corbels and orthostats in the passage at Newgrange.**

Above: **(Fig 19) Amorphous Close-area Picking on RS16, the cross lintel supporting the corbelled roof at Newgrange.**

sions and smoothen the corners by this form of picking. Similar picking occurs all along the passage and, again, the O'Kellys mentioned this but did not record it in detail. It occurs on many of the corbels and on most of the orthostats (Figure 18); up to 92 per cent of Close Area-picking at Newgrange occurs inside the tomb. A number of the orthostats were actually shaped to a certain extent by this style of picking. Thus, at Newgrange the Close Area-picking was clearly used to remove the irregular surfaces of the stones to smoothen them and partly to shape them. It is very different from the way Close Area-picking is used at Knowth where it occurs more in amorphous patches on the face of a stone; there, many of the stones have fresh surfaces and look like they have just been quarried. There is thus quite a difference in how the stones were treated in each place.

At Newgrange, we also found extensive picking on the face of a stone that O'Kelly called the cross lintel (RS16). It occurs in the (modern) tunnel that was built over the passage roof and is situated at the base of the corbelling, where the outside of the chamber corbelling comes down to meet the passage roof (O'Kelly 1982, fig. 22). This very sturdy lintel has pick dressing all over it except on the lower left corner (Figure 19). This feature had not been noted previously and it is important because there had been suggestions that pick dressing might be a later feature in the sequence of carvings, based on the way it obscures some of the carvings both inside the tomb and on the kerbstones; this picked stone is, however, located right in the heart of the monument and the picking must be an original feature, as indeed is the picking on the corbels inside the chamber. Close Area-picking is well known at several other iconic sites such as Maeshowe in the Orkney Islands (Thomas 2016) and the Dolmen de Soto in Andalucía, Spain (Bueno Ramirez *et al.* 2018). At Newgrange we also examined the kerbstones in detail and recorded Dispersed Picking on all the visible surfaces, a feature that has not been noted hitherto.

BEYOND IRELAND

Looking now at wider connections, one of the great treasures from Knowth is the small,

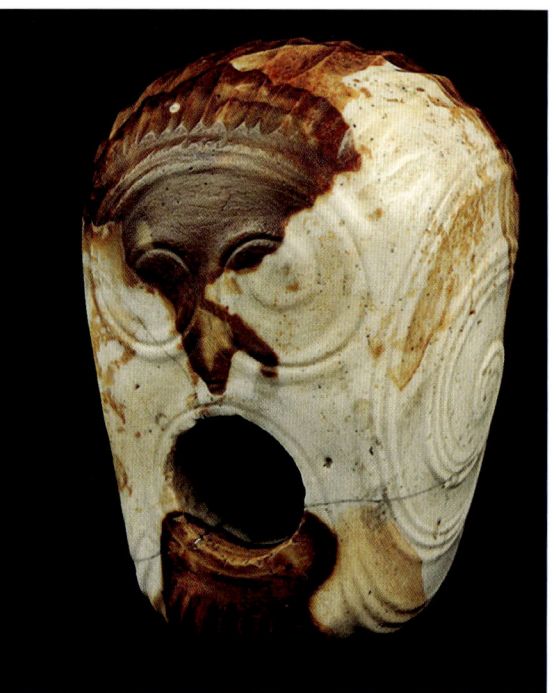

carved flint macehead that was found in the right-hand recess of Knowth 1 East, which can be seen in the National Museum of Ireland (Figure 20). The finely worked decoration includes panels of lozenges, and spirals, including a distinctive C-shaped spiral. This C-shaped spiral never occurs in Irish megalithic art but has been found in some passage tombs in the Orkney Islands, on the badly damaged passage tomb known as the Calderstones near Liverpool and on Temple Wood stone circle and some open-air rock art sites in Scotland. The macehead is of a type known as the Maesmor group, and is clearly not an Irish piece; it was probably brought in from Britain, although the exact source of this unusually coloured flint is not known (Shee Twohig 2022c).

Above: **(Fig 20) Maesmor type macehead from Knowth 1 East chamber, showing C-spiral motif.**

Opposite page: **(Fig 21) Carvings at Gavrinis passage tomb, Brittany.**

To look briefly further afield, megalithic art is found in Brittany and to a lesser extent in other parts of France and in Iberia. The sites there are mostly much earlier in date than the Irish sites and, in fact, the earliest carving was on large standing stones rather than on megalithic tombs, although many of the standing stones were later incorporated into megalithic tombs. There are clear connections between the French and Iberian art, with the use of a range of shared iconographic images that were clearly important to the people who carved, painted or observed them. The figurative images include items such as axes, crooks or throwing sticks, fertility symbols, and crescents that are interpreted as boats in Brittany and as neck ornaments in Alentejo. Prestige artefacts and raw materials such as jadeitite and variscite were exchanged between these areas. It is only in the later stages of the continental passage tomb sequence that the connections with Ireland can be seen, such as some simple geometric motifs; over time more geometric images were used in these areas including zigzags, serpentiforms and circles.

The carvings at Gavrinis in Brittany have long been compared to Irish art and the site has been radiocarbon dated to c.4200-4000 BC based on oak charcoal (Cassen *et al.* 2016). It has the only spirals recorded beyond Ireland and Britain and has iconographic carvings such as axes and a bow and an extensive series of arcs as well as the spirals (Figure 21). As already noted, similarities can be seen between some aspects of Knowth megalithic art and the art in the Breton angled-passage tombs,

which date to the same period but, for the most part, the Irish carvers seem to have gone their own way.

In Iberia, there is very good evidence of quite a lot of painted art in addition to carvings. One of the best-preserved examples, at Antelas in Viseu, Portugal, (Figure 22) is extensively painted with red and black motifs on a white background. Sometimes there is both carving and painting on the same stone. No definite evidence of painting has been found as yet in Irish megalithic tombs but it has been found both in tombs and contemporary settlements in the Orkney Islands (Bueno Ramirez *et al.* 2019) and it may well be discovered here in the future.

Above: **(Fig 22) Painting at Antelas passage tomb, Portugal.**

To conclude, it is clear that Boyne Valley megalithic art is exceptionally elaborate, with a far greater range of styles than elsewhere in Ireland. Perhaps the Boyne Valley art should be seen as evolving from earlier Standard Megalithic Art in the rest of the country. Irish (and British) carvings are very different from the art in Atlantic mainland Europe and seem to have undergone transformation during transmission from there, with only some of the later art in Atlantic Europe having slight parallels with the Irish art.

Acknowledgements

I would like to acknowledge all the contributors to the Knowth volume (Eogan and Shee Twohig 2022) on which much of this paper is based, in particular Dr Kerri Cleary, Robin Turk, Ken Williams, and Helena King as editor, and also the support provided by very many institutions to the Knowth project over a long period, especially the National Monuments Service, the Royal Irish Academy, the Heritage Council and Meath County Council. The recent Newgrange fieldwork was supported by the Directed Research for World Heritage Scheme Grant, administered through the Royal Irish Academy.

BIBLIOGRAPHY

Bueno Ramírez, P., Linares Catela, J. A., Balbín Behrmann, R. de, and Barroso Bermejo, R. (eds.) 2018. *Símbolos de la muerte en la prehistoria reciente del sur de Europa. El dolmen de Soto, Huelva, España*. Arqueología Monografías. Junta de Andalucía.

Bueno Ramírez, P., Balbín Behrmann, R. de, Barroso Bermejo, R., Laporte, L., Gouézin, P., Cousseau, F., Salanova, L., Card, N., Benetau, G., Mens, E., Sheridan, A., Carrera Ramírez, F., Hernanz, A., Iriarte, M. and Steelman, K. 2019. From pigment to symbol: The role of paintings in the ideological construction of European megaliths *IN*: Müller, J., Hinz, M. and Wunderlich, M. (eds.) *Megaliths – Societies – Landscapes: Early Monumentality and Social Differentiation in Neolithic Europe*. Bonn: Habelt Verlag, pp845–865.

Cassen, S., Grimaud, V., Lescop, L., Robinet, E. and Marcoux, N. 2016. Étude sur un monolithe – la dalle S12 au sol du monument de Gavrinis (Larmor-Baden, Morbihan). *Revue archéologique de l'Ouest*. 33, pp55–76.

Eogan, G. and Cleary, K. 2017. *Excavations at Knowth Volume 6: The Passage Tomb Archaeology of the Great Mound at Knowth*. Dublin: Royal Irish Academy.

Eogan, G. and Shee Twohig, E. 2022. *Excavations at Knowth 7: The Megalithic Art of the Passage Tombs at Knowth, County Meath*. Dublin: Royal Irish Academy.

Hensey, R. and Robin, G. 2011. More than meets the eye: new recordings of megalithic art in north-west Ireland. *Oxford Journal of Archaeology* 30, pp109–130.

O'Kelly, C. 1978. *Illustrated guide to Newgrange and the other Boyne monuments* (3rd edn). Blackrock, Co. Cork: C. O'Kelly.

O'Kelly, M.J. 1982. *Newgrange: archaeology, art and legend*. London: Thames and Hudson.

O'Sullivan, M. 2004. Little and large: comparing Knockroe with Knowth *IN*: Roche, H., Grogan, E., Bradley, J., Coles, J. and Raftery, B. (eds.) *From megaliths to metals: essays in honour of George Eogan*. Oxford: Oxbow Books, pp44–56.

Shee Twohig, E. 1981. *The megalithic art of western Europe*. Oxford: Clarendon Press.

Shee Twohig, E. 2022a. Techniques and Motifs of Knowth Art *IN*: Eogan, G. and Shee Twohig, E. 2022. *Excavations at Knowth 7: The Megalithic Art of the Passage Tombs at Knowth, County Meath*. Dublin: Royal Irish Academy, pp61–123.

Shee Twohig, E. 2022b. Styles and Sculptures in Knowth Art *IN*: Eogan, G. and Shee Twohig, E. 2022. *Excavations at Knowth 7: The Megalithic Art of the Passage Tombs at Knowth, County Meath*. Dublin: Royal Irish Academy. pp125–189.

Shee Twohig, E. 2022c. Knowth Art in Context *IN*: Eogan, G. and Shee Twohig, E. 2022. *Excavations at Knowth 7: The Megalithic Art of the Passage Tombs at Knowth, County Meath*. Dublin: Royal Irish Academy, pp191–257.

Shee Twohig, E. and Cleary, K. 2022. Introduction *IN*: Eogan, G. and Shee Twohig, E. 2022. *Excavations at Knowth 7: The Megalithic Art of the Passage Tombs at Knowth, County Meath*. Dublin: Royal Irish Academy, pp1-34.

Thomas, A. 2016. *Art and architecture in Neolithic Orkney: process, temporality and context*. Oxford: Archaeopress.

Williams, K. 2023. Echoes of the Neolithic at Irish Stone Circles: the discovery of megalithic art at Grange Stone Circle, Co. Limerick. *Archaeology Ireland* 37, pp30-35.

Chapter 6:

Professor George Eogan was a veritable colossus of Irish archaeology who was unfailingly kind and generous to me. He is very, very much missed.

DR ALISON SHERIDAN

Ireland in the Wider Prehistoric World, 4300 – 1750 BC

Dr Alison Sheridan's research and publications are largely concerned with the Neolithic, Chalcolithic and the Bronze Age of Ireland and Britain. She has a special expertise in ceramics, stone axeheads and jewellery made of jet, amber, gold and faience. Here she explores the extent and nature of Ireland's connections with the wider world in the Neolithic, Chalcolithic and Early Bronze Age.

In considering the wider world in which Ireland's Neolithic, Chalcolithic and Early Bronze Age inhabitants lived and the many and varied ways in which their lives were intertwined with those of people across the water, there is no better way to start than with this wonderful stone object found outside the western passage tomb in the main monument

---

Left: Newgrange (left), Knowth and Dowth, and other huge passage tombs in Ireland, represent the culmination of a centuries-long process of monumental aggrandizement.

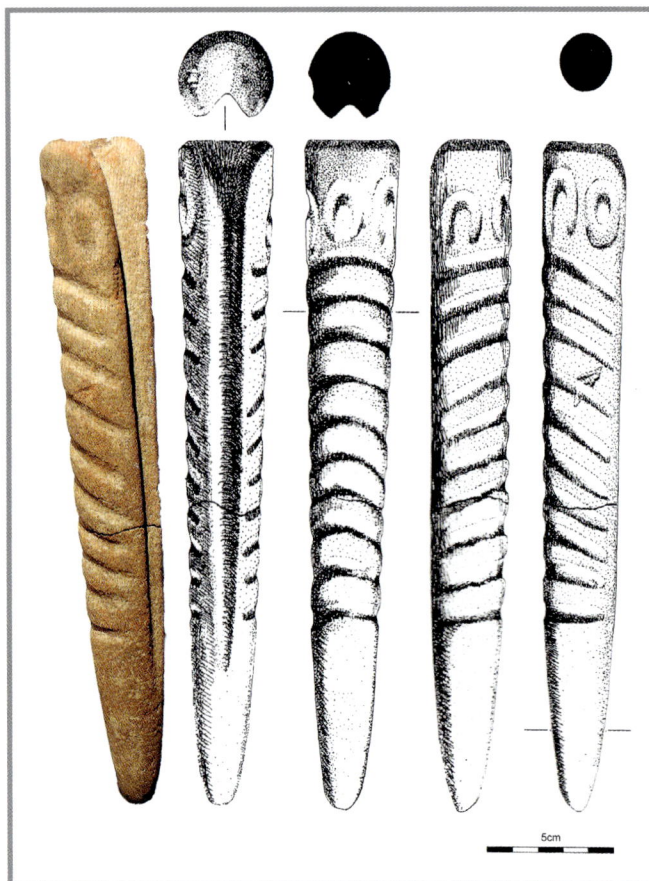

at Knowth, the so-called 'idol'. It was George Eogan (Eogan 1980) who realized that this particular phallic object, which arguably could be a stylized representation of a divine being, may have travelled over 1,500 kilometres, since

Above: **The carved stone 'idol' found outside the western passage of the main mound at Knowth, similar to objects from the Tagus estuary in Portugal.**

the closest and, indeed, the only *comparanda* are to be found in Portugal around the mouth of the Tagus River where Lisbon is now.

This discovery is one of many that remind us just how sophisticated, well-connected and navigationally skilled were the people who were responsible for building the major passage tombs of Brú na Bóinne. The reason behind this extraordinarily long-distance movement relates to the specific power politics at the time around 3200 BC, in which the undertaking of long and perilous sea journeys and the bringing back of exotic ideas, objects and practices was a fundamental part of the strategy of maintaining and enhancing the power of the elite – a topic that will be considered further in this paper.

This was just one of the many different ways in which the lives of Ireland's inhabitants were connected to those of people across the sea over the two and a half millennia from around 4300 BC to around 1750 BC. In this broad-brush review of the evidence, I hope to give little snapshots or case studies highlighting who or what was travelling, from where to where, and why.

FARMING

The first case study concerns the way in which the farming way of life came to be established in Ireland.

The sedentary way of life featuring the production of food using domesticated animals and plants was fundamentally different from that of Ireland's indigenous Mesolithic inhabitants who relied on exploiting wild resources through hunting, fishing and foraging, moving around the landscape as particular resources came into season. There has been debate about how farming came to Ireland and Britain with some, including myself, arguing that it was introduced by immigrant farming groups from the Continent, while others hold that Ireland's Mesolithic inhabitants chose to adopt it, having made regular trips to the Continent where they witnessed this 'weird' new way of

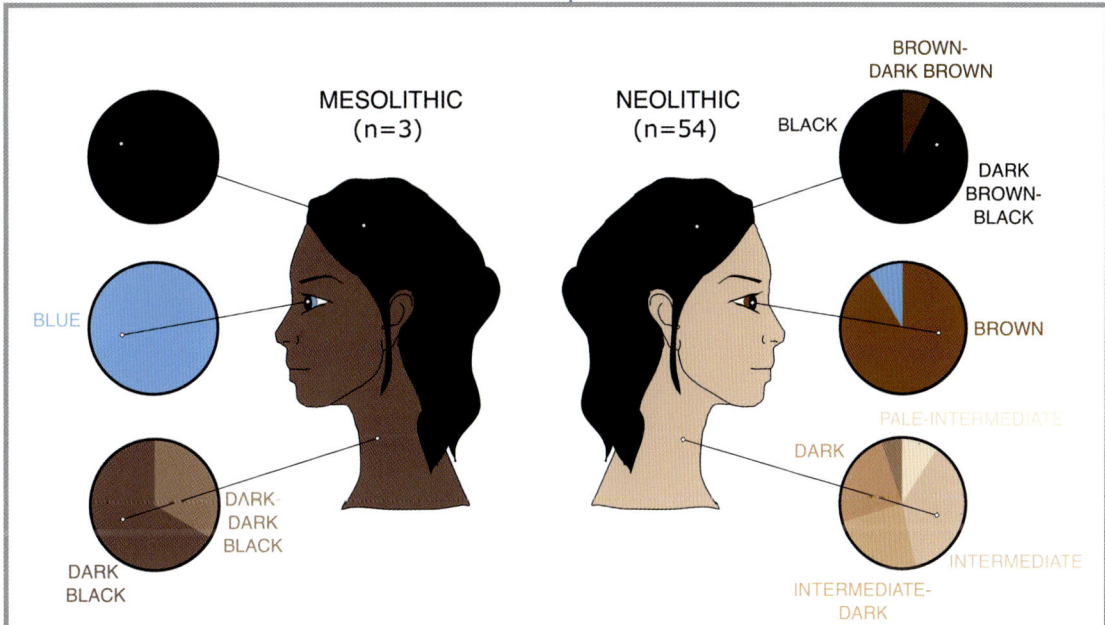

DNA evidence shows the spread of farming groups to Ireland in the Early Neolithic, bringing a different way of life from that of the Mesolithic inhabitants. *(Above)* differences in appearance; *(next page)* maps showing the changing genetic makeup of Britain and Ireland with the arrival of farming groups.

PIGMENTATION FIGURE:
The illustration above shows predicted pigmentation profiles for Mesolithic individuals in Ireland and Britain as obtained using the HIrisPlex-S system (as discussed in Cassidy *et al.* 2020). The pie charts show the frequencies of predicted hair, eye and skin colour in the Mesolithic *(left)* and Neolithic *(right)*, with the most common colour shown on the reconstructed individuals. The three Mesolithic samples were all predicted to have "Dark Brown–Black" hair and "Dark–Dark Black" to "Dark Black" skin, with blue eye colouring (although these results should be treated with caution). In the Neolithic, hair shades ranging from "Black" to "Brown–Dark Brown" and skin colours ranging from "Dark–Dark Black" to "Pale–Intermediate" are predicted, with mostly brown eye colouring.

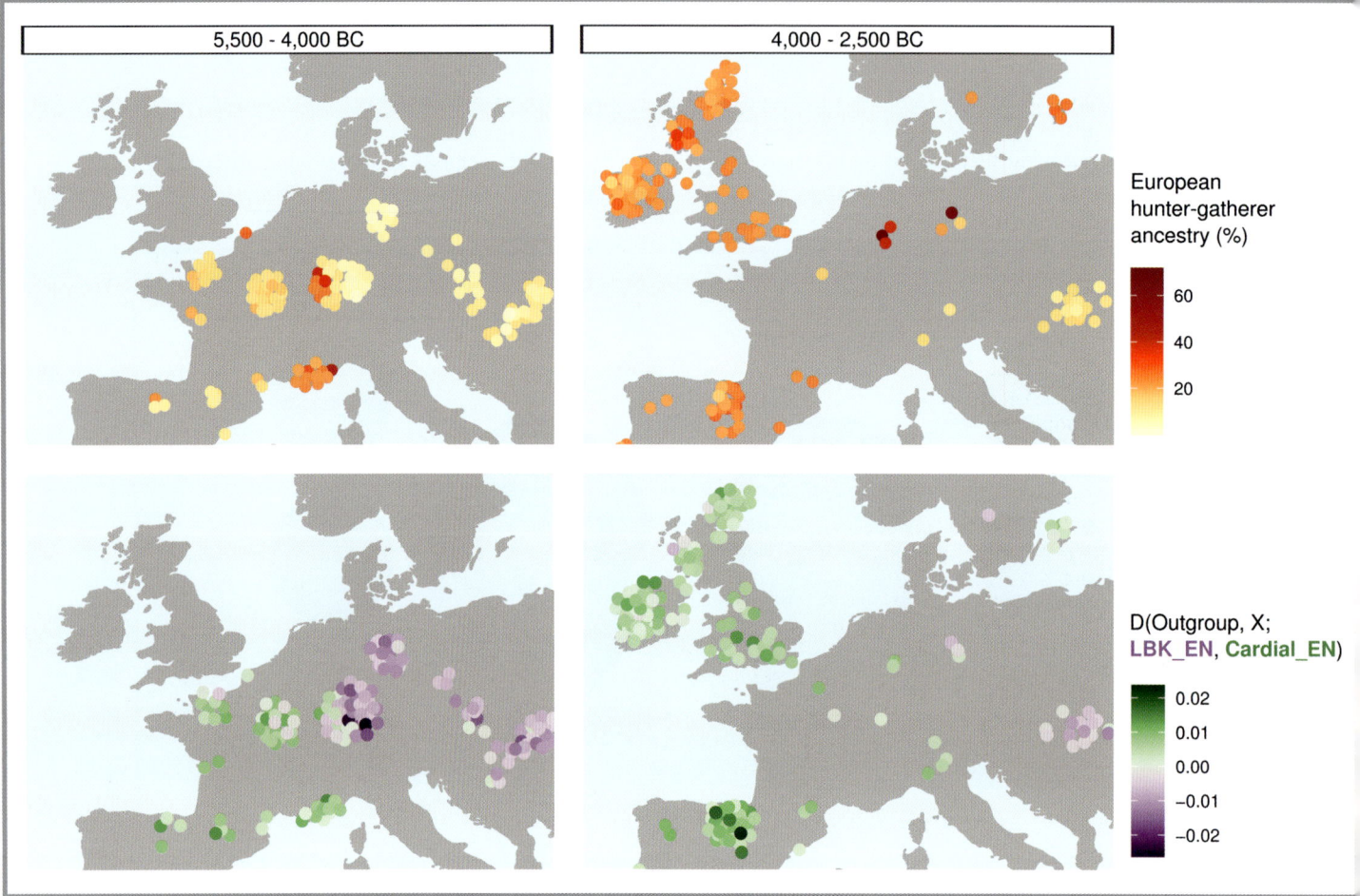

life that contrasted so starkly with their own.

The only thing on which the different proponents can agree is that the 'nuts and bolts' of farming they used, the domesticated cattle, sheep, goats and pigs, and the wheat, barley and flax, must have been physically transported over the sea from the Continent, as the wild progenitors of most of these species simply do not exist in Ireland. We know, also, that the wild boar that did exist were not domesticated here.

The same goes for the practice of making pottery – this was a continental technology wholly alien to Mesolithic Ireland – and for other aspects of the Neolithic way of life.

Thanks to the recent work on ancient DNA carried out by Lara Cassidy and Dan Bradley (Cassidy *et al.* 2020) in Trinity College Dublin and by their colleagues elsewhere, the answer to the question of how farming arrived in Ireland is now plain to see. We are indeed dealing with the arrival of immigrant farming communities from the Continent, many of whom probably looked different from Ireland's indigenous inhabitants by being slightly lighter in skin colour and having differently coloured eyes.

Moreover, Cassidy and Bradley's genetic research (ibid.) has concluded that Irish Mesolithic communities were profoundly insular, their genetic signatures showing that effectively they had been cut off from Britain and the Continent for millennia. Their material culture and their funerary practices showed no sign whatsoever of interactions with elsewhere, with the possible sole exception of the Isle of Man. And so, the idea of Irish hunter-fisher-foragers regularly setting off in their boats to visit the Continent is not convincing. In contrast, if you look at what Continental farmers were getting up to during the fifth millennium BC in Brittany, there is plentiful evidence for long-distance deep-sea sailing.

My model of how farming came to be established in Ireland and Britain does not involve a single or, indeed, a massive episode of migration but rather several episodes or processes, differing in scale from each other, where variable numbers of farmers came from different parts of the northern half of France to different parts of our archipelago for different reasons, and with differing responses from the locals.

Opposite page: **Ancestral diversity across European Neolithic populations. Left and right panels show Europe before and after the Neolithization of Britain and Ireland (*circa*. 4,000 BC). In the top panels Neolithic individuals are coloured according to the approximate percentage of their ancestry derived from European hunter-gatherers. The bottom panels explore the relative contributions of the two main routes of Neolithic expansion to the same dataset of individuals. The Mediterranean route is represented by individuals from the north-eastern Spanish Neolithic (Cardial_EN) and the Central Europe route by early LBK samples (LBK_EN).**

Below: **The author's four-strand model of the spread of farming peoples in the Neolithic, three of which affected Ireland.**

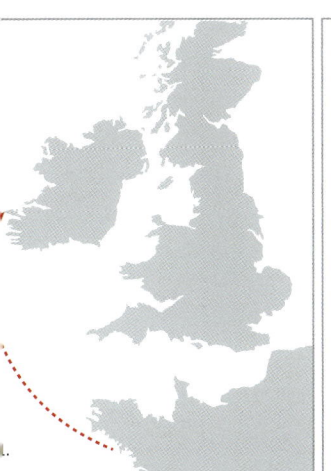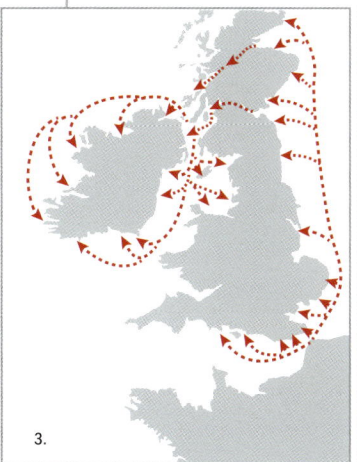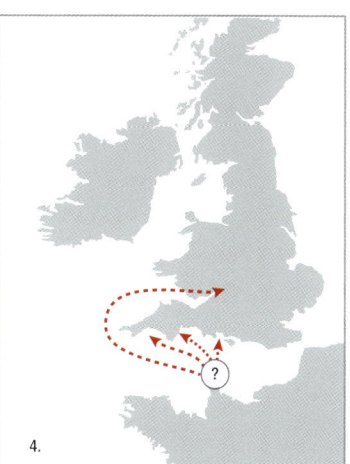

NEOLITHIC MIGRATION

Three strands of Neolithization through this process of migration can be inferred for Ireland. The first one *(page 115, panel 1)* seems to have been a bit of a false start and can be summarized in a nutshell (appropriately enough) like this. Picture the scene: it is a fine, sunny day around 4350 BC in the Mesolithic campsite at Ferriter's Cove in County Kerry. A few strangers had appeared in the area recently with some funny new animals that looked good to hunt and eat, which is just exactly what seems to have happened, resulting in the bones of domesticated cattle ending up in a hearth in that indigenous campsite.

In that instance, the indigenous people were not remotely interested in learning how to farm, and the incoming farmers from north-west France and their animals had not come over in sufficient numbers to constitute a critical mass so that they could establish themselves. And so, we see a very rapid end to the Neolithic in this part of Ireland at that particular time. This is a caricature, of course, but I have not come across a more plausible reading of the Ferriter's Cove evidence.

The second strand of Neolithization, arriving from the Morbihan area of Brittany *(page 115, panel 2)* around 4000 BC, brought to the coastal areas around the northern half of Ireland and to western Britain the Breton Neolithic tradition of burying the dead in megalithic funerary monuments. In Ireland and Scotland, the simple, small monuments that are seen opposite stand at the beginning of long and complex sequences of passage tomb evolution that in Ireland culminated in the massive passage tombs of Brú na Bóinne

and elsewhere.

Confirmation that people were coming indeed from Brittany is found not just in the design and architecture of these monuments but also by the distinctive, Breton-style Late Castellic bowl that was found in the monument at Achnacreebeag on the west coast of Scotland. Its shape, its rainbow motif and its fringe on the upper belly can all be matched in the Morbihan area of southern Brittany. As for why people should have upped sticks in Brittany to sail northwards to an unknown

Left: **Closed megalithic chambers and simple passage tombs built by the second strand of immigrant farmers from Brittany around 4000 BC.**

Above right: **Breton-style late Castellic pot found at the Achnacreebeag monument in western Scotland.**

Opposite page: **Artist's impression of Ferriter's Cove Mesolithic landscape when the first Neolithic farming people arrived but failed to establish themselves.**

destination, we have to consider the changes that had been going on in Breton society in preceding centuries, with the collapse around 4300 BC of one, very macho, social system based on the dominance of a few so-called 'god kings', to use Serge Cassen's (Cassen *et al.* 2011) term, and its replacement by a different social order. It is not possible to discuss this in detail here but Serge Cassen has written at length on this topic.

The third strand of Neolithization featured the arrival, ultimately from Nord-Pas-de-Calais but probably via northern Britain, of different groups of immigrant farmers from northern France apparently coming in considerable numbers (Figure 5, panel 3). This movement was ultimately occasioned by population pressure and build-up in the Paris Basin, which from 4300 BC onwards led to people expanding out from there, with some going to Nord-Pas-de-Calais and thence, eventually, to Britain and Ireland. The DNA data back up this scenario.

These people dealt with their dead by placing a few, select members of the community within timber mortuary structures and also by cremating them in the open air. Both of these practices are represented in the north of Ireland, with Dooey's Cairn at Ballymacaldrack, County Antrim, being Ireland's only example of a timber mortuary structure. These mortuary structures, of which numerous examples have been found in Britain, were often fronted by curving timber façades and were eventually encased in long rectangular or trapezoidal-shaped mounds, often after burning down the structure. These were the origins of both court tombs and portal tombs in Ireland, I would argue. These incomers also brought the tradition of building rectangular houses. The huge, communal versions that can be seen in Scotland and England were probably built by several immigrant farming families when they moved into a new area; they would stay there until they

---

Below: **Artist's reconstruction of timber mortuary structure with facade from the Early Neolithic; this example is Street House, NE England.**

Opposite page: **Two of the Irish axeheads made from rock from the north Italian Alps (both jadeitite), Raymoghy (Kincraigy) Co Donegal** *(above),* **and Paslickstown, Co Westmeath,** *(below).*

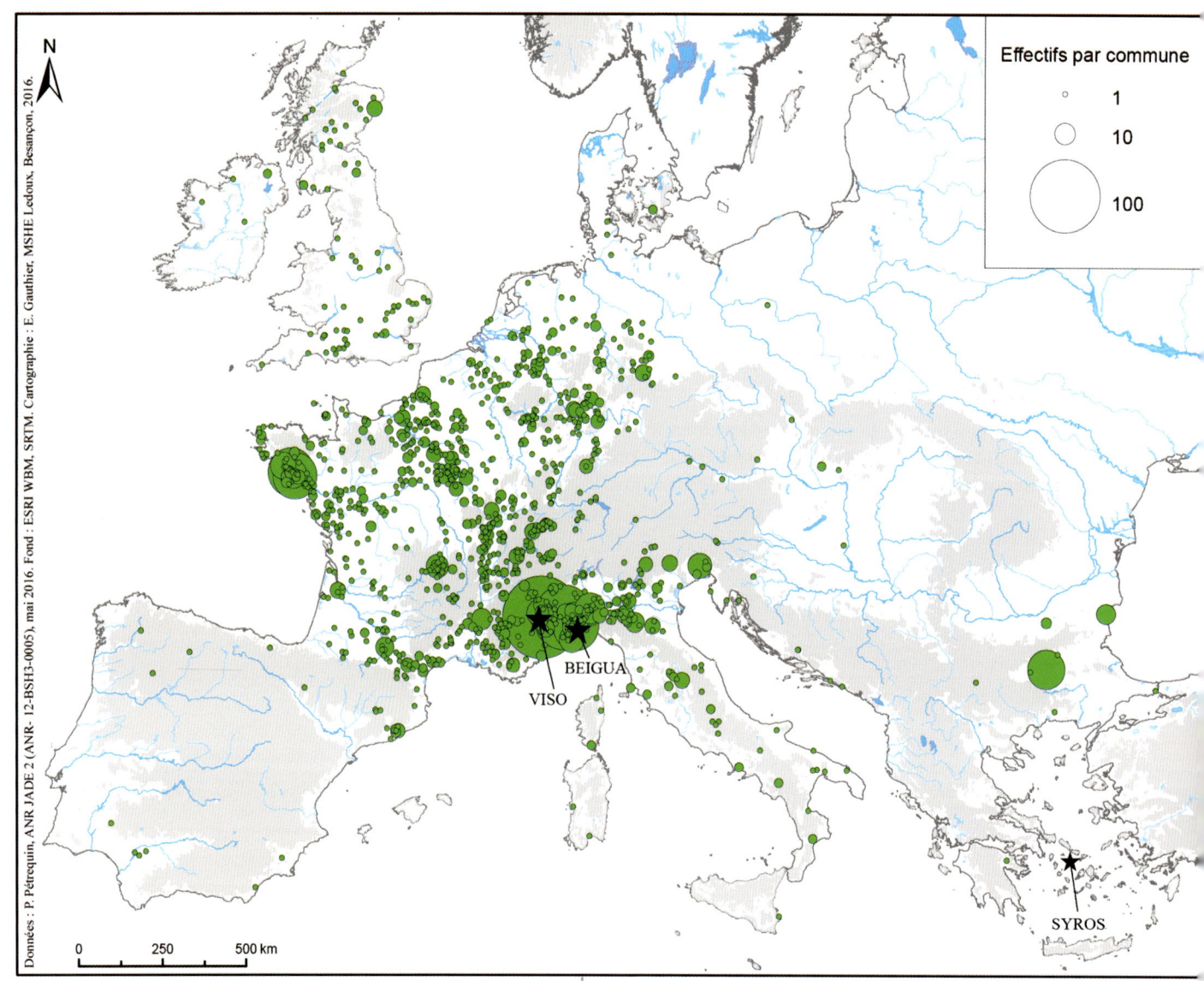

felt sufficiently well established to bud off into individual farmsteads. In County Sligo, there is evidence suggesting that these immigrants were present from around 4100 BC, and within a few generations there were enough of them to build a large enclosure (probably used for communal gatherings, as well as other purposes) at Magheraboy.

Among the Continental novelties brought by these people were superb axeheads made from jadeitite, originating in the north Italian Alps. A small fragment of a deliberately broken axehead was discovered by Ros Ó Maoldúin at Treanbaun in County Galway recently. These were not just everyday axeheads for chopping down trees. Rather, they were precious, sacred objects, 'green treasures from the magic mountains far away', which were used in a purely ceremonial way, before being returned to the world of the ancestors and gods, by placing them in watery areas, for example.

Thanks to a major international French-led research project, *Projet JADE*, we know exactly where they originated. We know also that they would have been old, up to several centuries old, when they were deposited in Ireland. The map by *Projet JADE* (*opposite*) shows the source areas to have been on Monte Viso near Turin and Monte Beigua above Genoa and charts the distribution of large axeheads of jadeitite and other Alpine rocks right across Europe. Neolithic people may well have associated mountains with the gods, believing that objects made from mountain rock were imbued with special divine powers. The axe-

Opposite page: **The distribution of Neolithic axeheads originating in the north Italian Alps.**

Above: **Block of jadeitite and, beyond, the peak of Monte Viso, one of the two source areas of jadeitite axeheads.**

Right: **Complete axe with head of Antrim porcellanite, found at Shulishader on the Isle of Lewis in the Outer Hebrides.**

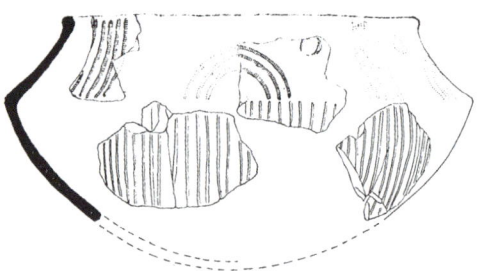

Ballymacaldrack, County Antrim

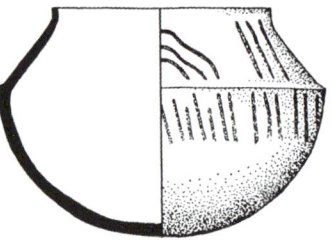

Beacharra, Argyll & Bute

Antrim porcellanite, exemplifies this kind of interaction. It shows that the existence of the sea was not a barrier to the extensive networks of social interaction that were established rapidly by the Neolithic farmers and over which desirable things, resources, people and ideas circulated.

Particularly close links can be seen between north-east Ireland and south-west Scotland despite the fact that the currents in the North Channel can be treacherous. We can see these links, for example, in the shared design of the megalithic monuments that are known as Clyde cairns in south-west Scotland and as court tombs in Ireland. These represent a translation into stone of the timber monuments that have been discussed before. We know from radiocarbon dating programmes that they came into being around 3750 BC on both sides of the Irish Sea.

Other evidence for these close links includes items of Antrim flint that have been found in south-west Scotland, as in the magnificent hoard found near Campbeltown on the Kintyre peninsula; in finds in north-east Ireland of pitchstone (a volcanic glass) from the Isle of Arran; and in the design of the pottery that is found in several court tombs and in Clyde cairns. Interestingly, these dec-

heads found in Ireland would have travelled up to 1,800 kilometres from their sources during their long lives, but not directly. They would have circulated for some time in northern France before being brought over from there by the pioneering farming groups as precious communal heirlooms. Some of them were polished to a glassy sheen to maximize their magical protective powers, which would have been needed during the risky sea crossing from the Continent.

SEA CONNECTIONS

The second case study is focused on the regular 'toing and froing' across and around and up and down the Irish Sea and adjacent stretches of water by these farming communities throughout much of the fourth millennium. The axe from Shulishader in the Outer Hebrides (page 121), with its axehead of

Opposite page: **Hoard of Antrim flint items found at Auchenhoan, near Campbeltown, Scotland** *(above),* **Arran pitchstone in north-east Ireland** *(below left),* **and shared pottery designs** *(below right),* **all evidence of close sea links.**

Above: **Portal tombs in Ireland, Wales and Cornwall show early connections around the Irish Sea: Dyffryn Ardudwy portal tomb, Wales.** © Niall Sharples.

orated bowls with their rainbow motifs are the ceramic descendants of the Breton Late Castellic bowl from Achnacreebeag that was discussed earlier.

As noted above, there is evidence for more far-flung contact to the north as well, linking Ireland to the Hebrides, several days' sail away, in the form of sherds of Hebridean-style jars found on the sandhills of Portstewart, County Derry/Londonderry, and by the Antrim porcellanite axeheads found at Shulishader on Lewis and elsewhere in Scotland. The sources of this particular rock are Tievebulliagh mountain, a prominent peak in the Glens of Antrim, and Brockley on Rathlin Island.

Further south, there is plentiful evidence for connections across the Irish Sea to Wales and to south-west England as can be seen, for example, in the distribution of portal tombs, a distinctive type of megalithic monument whose origins, like those of court tombs, can be traced back to the timber mortuary structures of the earliest Neolithic. Although the Cornish and Welsh ones are poorly dated, we know, thanks to work carried out by Dr Ann Lynch (Lynch 2014), that Poulnabrone portal tomb was in use as early as around 3800 BC. There were, of course, connections also with north-west England and the Isle of Man as shown, for instance, in the axeheads made of tuff from Great Langdale in Cumbria that ended up in Ireland.

Opposite page: **Evolution of passage tombs in Co. Sligo from simple structures** *(top,* **Carrowmore 7***)* **to increasingly aggrandized monuments** *(centre,* **Listoghil, Carrowmore***),* **culminating in Queen Maeve's Cairn on Knocknarea** *(bottom).*

ELITE TRAVEL

My third case study, about the external connections of the people responsible for the construction of the major passage tombs of Brú na Bóinne, takes us on several very long journeys and introduces us to the concept of elite travel for the purposes of what the anthropologist Mary Helms (Helms 1988) has referred to as 'cosmological acquisition'. This term describes how certain privileged people used to undertake heroic long-distance journeys to bring back esoteric knowledge and exotic objects as part of an elite power play to underline their own importance and to 'get one over on their rivals'.

To cut a very long and complex story short, essentially Newgrange, Knowth and Dowth, and other huge passage tombs in Ireland, represent the culmination of a centuries-long process of monumental aggrandizement. It was a case of competitive conspicuous consumption on constructing monuments to house the dead, whereby the leading groups in Neolithic society vied to create the most splendid and imposing monument for the members of their family or group, in whichever way kinship was constituted. We can see this process, for example, if we compare the small and simple Early Neolithic megalithic tombs of the Carrowmore cemetery near Sligo town with the massive Queen Maeve's Cairn on the summit of Knocknarea mountain, overlooking that earlier cemetery and dominating the landscape. Queen Maeve's Cairn could have been roughly contemporary with the Brú na Bóinne mega-passage tombs.

I and others have suggested in the past

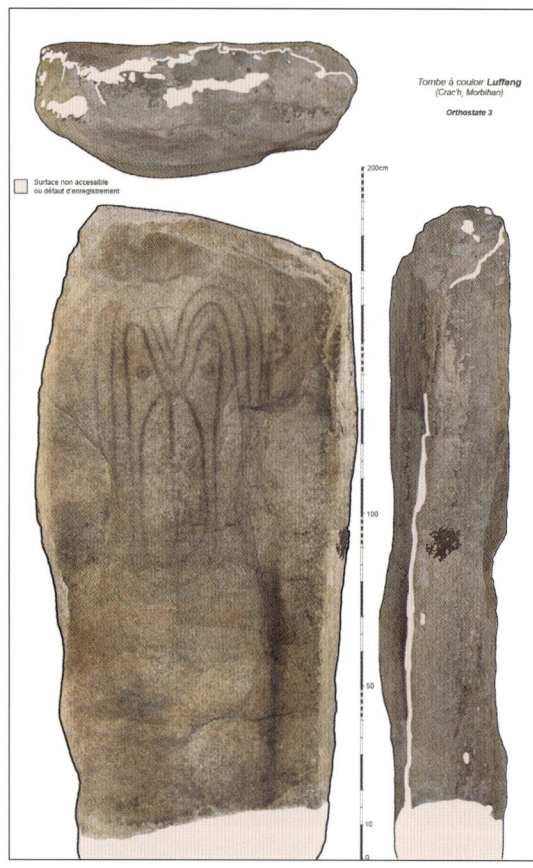

that this process of aggrandizement reflected an increasingly inegalitarian society, not least because the amassing of materials and labour to build a massive passage tomb – and at Newgrange, the designing of the monument so that the rays of the rising sun would

---

'Guardian goddess' figures from Le Luffang, Brittany *(above)* and Knowth West *(right)*.

run along the passage and into the chamber at midwinter solstice – would have required very careful planning, leadership and organization.

Although it has become fashionable in some quarters to play down the notion of elites in Irish and British Neolithic society, I personally find it incomprehensible that monuments such as the massive passage tombs at Newgrange, Knowth and Dowth could have been built as the communal project of an egalitarian society. Interestingly, support for the idea of aggrandized passage tombs being an expression of elite power comes from the genetic work recently undertaken by Cassidy *et al.* 2020. One of their key findings is that within Ireland there were familial links between passage tomb builders across long distances and over many generations. This could indeed suggest that the building of aggrandized passage tombs was the preserve of a narrow spectrum of Neolithic society.

Moreover, at Newgrange, the concept of 'keeping it in the family' was taken to the extreme with the burial of a man who was the offspring of an incestuous coupling. Marrying within the family is a known strategy of different kinds of elite around the world and across time and, indeed, is not unknown among western aristocracies in the more recent past! As a strategy, incest is one way of maintaining the purity of the bloodline.

It would appear that around 3200/3100 BC, the power-play strategy of the groups responsible for constructing the three major Brú na Bóinne monuments involved travelling to the Morbihan area of southern Brittany, and even further afield down to Iberia, to visit the megalithic funerary monuments there, to join in the seasonal celebrations and acquire esoteric knowledge and exotica to bring home. We can see this, for example, in the way that the western tomb of Knowth featured the addition of a long passage with a slight angle to what probably had been a small pre-existing passage tomb. This made it

---

Above: **Comparative plans of Knowth West** *(top)* **and Le Luffang with the positions of the 'Guardian goddess' stones indicated by stars.**

Opposite page: **A similar style of high-relief megalithic art is found at tombs in Brú na Bóinne** *(top)* **and in the older passage tomb of Gavrinis, Morbihan, Brittany** *(bottom)*.

resemble the *allées coudées* (angled passage tombs) of the Morbihan area and there can be little doubt that it was a quite deliberate design feature and emulation of Breton monuments, rather than a chance misalignment of the passage and chamber, (See Shee Twohig p100).

We can also see an example of this practice in the very striking and very distinctive so-called 'guardian goddess' figure located at the entrance to the chamber at Knowth West. This arguably resembles similar figures found in the angled passage tombs of Le Luffang and Les Pierres Plates in the Morbihan. It may be that the design in all three monuments features a more or less

abstract image of a vulva with eyes above it, suggesting that a powerful female deity is represented.

A third feature that suggests that those responsible for building the mega-monuments in Brú na Bóinne had seen the passage tombs of the Morbihan area is the dense, high-relief style of megalithic art that is particularly prominent at Newgrange. Similarly dense and high-relief designs can be seen on the passage tomb of Gavrinis, Morbihan *(page 129)*, which would have been several centuries old by the time a grandee from Brú na Bóinne visited it.

Moreover, as noted at the beginning of this

Above: **The interior design of Newgrange passage tomb was replicated in the Orkney Islands at Maeshowe.**

chapter, the long-distance voyaging of the Brú na Bóinne elite extended as far as Iberia, as can be seen from the tiny, foot-shaped carved pebble from Newgrange that finds its parallels among the Argalo-type idols of north-west Spain and by the aforementioned ribbed 'idol' from Knowth whose parallels are to be found around the mouth of the Tagus in Portugal.

It is clear that news of the Brú na Bóinne mega-passage tombs spread far and wide, and they became magnets for what we might term 'pilgrimages', in which privileged members of society from elsewhere got to join in the religious ceremonies and partake of their own cosmological acquisition. We can see this in Wales, for example, at Barclodiad y Gawres on Anglesey, where an Irish-style passage tomb, complete with Irish passage tomb art and Irish-style bone pins, was built. Also on Anglesey, at Llanbedrgoch, a highly-decorated pot with features reminiscent of the Irish 'Carrowkeel bowl' style was found.

People from Scotland were also drawn to Brú na Bóinne, copying the sacred spiral symbol on some of their carved stone balls such as the one found at Towie in Aberdeenshire. The spiral design has also turned up on a different kind of symbol of power, an antler macehead, found as far away as Norfolk in eastern England. This appropriation of exotic and esoteric symbols is a classic aspect of this power-play strategy that we saw in play in Ireland, and it was very much part of the social dynamics in Orkney. We can assume that some of the practices and beliefs that went along with the symbols were also emulated. If, as seems likely at least to me, the spiral motif was a symbolic representation of the sun's eternal movement across the sky – with the arc of its daily journey from rising to setting spiralling outwards to midsummer and inwards to midwinter – then it is reasonable to assume that the ceremonies that were adopted by the visitors to Brú na Bóinne also focused on the solstices (and in particular, the winter solstice).

It is in Orkney that we see the most ostentatious example of cosmological acquisition involving visits to Brú na Bóinne. The prosperous and ambitious farmers on that archipelago, like the Irish passage tomb builders, had been engaging in a process of competitive conspicuous consumption focused on the building of bigger and better monuments for their dead since at least as early as 3500 BC. News of the amazing Brú na Bóinne monuments would have reached Orkney thanks to their extensive network of contacts, which linked Orkney with Ireland via the Outer Hebrides and other areas on Scotland's Atlantic coast. The Orkney elite evidently made the winning move in their competitive monument-building process by making the long sea journey to Brú na Bóinne and then replicating Newgrange at Maeshowe, complete with its cruciform chamber, long passage and orientation on the mid-winter sun. However, at Maeshowe it is the setting sun, rather than the rising sun, that was targeted, probably due to the local topography.

The ambitious elite of Orkney built similar passage tombs elsewhere on that archipelago too and included Irish passage tomb designs, albeit giving the spiral a distinctively Orcadian twist, to create the so-called 'horned spiral'. The spiral appeared yet again in Orkney on the distinctive Grooved Ware pottery that was

in use there, as on a famous sherd from Skara Brae, whose design resembles that seen on the kerbstone at the rear of Newgrange opposite the entrance. Orcadians also emulated the smooth stone balls seen in Irish passage tombs.

Above: **The Stones of Stenness, a novel monument type in Orkney.**

Opposite page: **Carved stone objects from Orkney that were both symbols of power and death-dealing weapons.**

The Orkney elite did not make long-distance voyages just to Brú na Bóinne. Thanks to ancient DNA analysis of the humble Orkney vole (*microtus arvalis Orcadensis*), we can say that they also sailed as far as the Continent, probably France or Spain, bringing voles back on the boat as a handy and self-replenishing food supply for the sea journey: voles breed rapidly. We know that people did eat them because the vole bones from Skara Brae showed the charring of their extremities that is typical of being stuck on a

invented a whole new kind of monument – the stone circle enclosed by a henge – at the Stones of Stenness, and they probably erected timber circles too. They invented a new style of pottery, flat-based Grooved Ware. They wore ostentatious chunky jewellery made from materials such as sperm whale ivory and whale bone. Their clothing pins may constitute an Orcadian twist on the long pins of bone and antler seen in Irish passage tombs. They made also an array of weird and wonderful carved stone objects that were arguably both symbols of power – weapons of social exclusion – and actual weapons. We know this because there are skulls from Cuween passage tomb in Orkney that had been hit with an object of this kind of size.

To judge from the amazing site of the Ness of Brodgar near Maeshowe and the Stones of Stenness, it is clear that Orkney became a magnet for pilgrimages in its own right, rivalling and perhaps even eclipsing Brú na Bóinne. The enormous stone-roofed houses found there may well have accommodated visiting dignitaries from far and wide and there is a huge pile of waste from their feasting. The range of items found at the Ness of Brodgar includes exotica such as Arran pitchstone. Clearly, the visitors took away with them the idea of making Grooved Ware, of building stone (and probably timber) circles and of using Orcadian designs.

The map (page 134) traces just one aspect of this rapid spread of Orkney influence down the west coast of Scotland. This southward spread of Grooved Ware pottery and of other features of Orkney elite life is truly astonishing, extending as far as Cornwall, Kent and south-west Ireland. We can even see

stick and roasted over a fire. We also know from finds of dog coprolites (faeces) that dogs were also eating Orkney voles.

It is clear that these ambitious Orcadian farmers succeeded in creating a new world order featuring themselves on top. They

Orcadian influence in Brú na Bóinne with, for example, a classic, early Orcadian-style Grooved Ware pot having been found along with a miniature Orkney-style macehead in Tomb 6 at Knowth *(page 26)*, accompanying cremated bone that has been radiocarbon-dated to 3100–2900 cal BC. We can also see it in the small siltstone plaque with an Orcadian-style lozenge design found in the eastern tomb at Knowth. Similar designs can

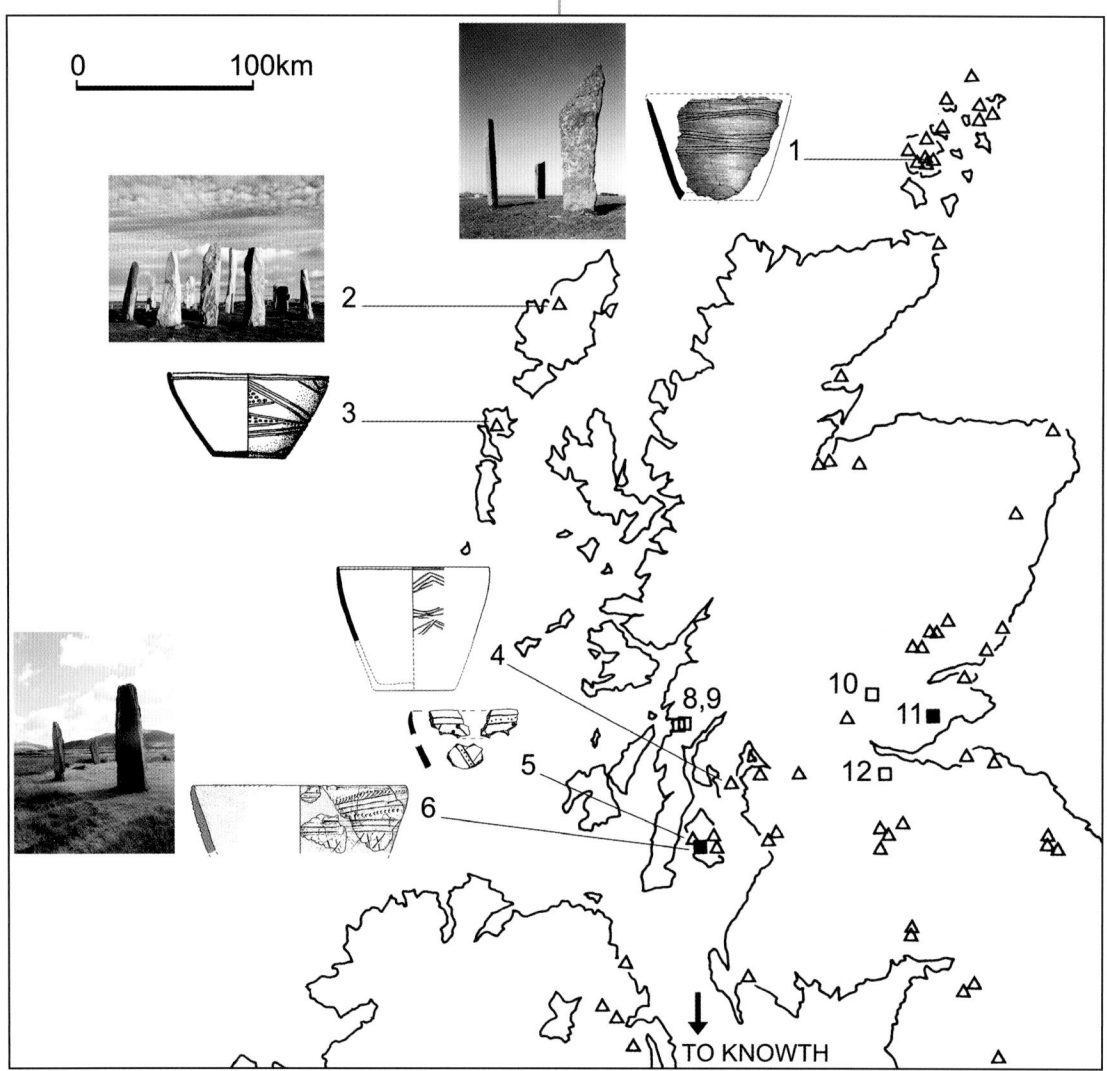

134

be seen at the settlement of Skara Brae on mainland Orkney. Most strikingly, it can be seen also in the two tiny beads found at Knowth that are miniature versions of Scottish six-knobbed carved stone balls like the one from the Ness of Brodgar.

It also seems likely that the practice of using stone maceheads was adopted in Ireland thanks to these connections with the Orkney elite, as can be seen from the pestle macehead found in the western tomb at Knowth and the miniature macehead pendants from Tara. Maceheads were certainly being made at the Ness of Brodgar and deliberately broken in Orkney as part of the religious ceremonies there. It is significant that the Knowth macehead was deliberately broken and indeed burnt in an echo of the Orcadian practice.

The most intriguing and iconic object in Brú na Bóinne is the superlative flint macehead from the eastern tomb at Knowth. Its design, I would argue, includes both the Orcadian horned spiral and also an Irish-style spiral. Even though flint of this size and quality does not occur naturally in Orkney, I do wonder whether it was actually made in Orkney using imported flint and presented as a diplomatic gift to a visiting person of high status from Brú na Bóinne during a visit to the Ness of Brodgar, to be displayed back home and deposited in a 'VIP' funerary context as a precious exotic treasure. We will never know but it is a possibility.

ATLANTIC LINKS

To give a sense of the changing ways in which Ireland was connected to the outside world, I move to case study four. This concerns Atlantic cup and ring rock art that is found unevenly distributed on stretches of living rock and on boulders at various locations on the Atlantic façade from northern Scotland to north-west Spain. This is not connected with Grooved Ware designs and there is much that still needs to be understood about its relationship, if any, with passage tomb art. Although its dating is not conclusive, there is a reasonable chance that it dates to the first half of the third millennium BC. What it does show is the continuation or a re-establishment of connections along the Atlantic façade and a sharing of ritual practices and beliefs, as work both by Joana

Above: **Bead found at Knowth is a miniature replica of a Scottish carved stone ball like the one found at the Ness of Brodgar.**

Opposite page: **The southward spread of Grooved Ware (triangles) and of stone circles (squares) along Scotland's Atlantic facade.**

Valdez-Tullett (Valdez-Tullett 2019) and Richard Bradley (Bradley 2022) has confirmed.

Additional confirmation of a Galician link was recently discovered at Dunchraigaig in Kilmartin Glen in west Scotland where a unique stretch of bedrock decorated with Galician-style deer designs was found reused in an Early Bronze Age cist.

NEW ARRIVALS AROUND 2400 BC

Dial forward to around 2400 BC and links with the Continent are strengthened as Ireland is drawn into the world of the so-called 'Beaker People'. This was when the use of Beaker pottery – a distinctive, Continental style of pottery – and the use of copper and gold were expanding. We know from DNA work in Britain that Beaker users were arriving from different parts of the Continent to different parts of Britain. It is likely that new people from the Continent were indeed arriving in Ireland. These included metal prospectors and miners of copper. They opened a copper mine on Ross Island in County Kerry, and it is thought that they probably came from somewhere along the Atlantic façade. Intriguingly, recent genetic research into the origins of the strawberry tree in Ireland (Sheehy Skeffington and Scott 2022) has indicated that it came from northern Spain, and it has been suggested that the Beaker-using copper miners from there introduced it around 2400 BC.

All the evidence points towards people

coming from the Atlantic façade rather than from central and northern Europe, which explains why Ireland has next to no individual Beaker graves like the ones that are so common in Britain. Indeed, we may be dealing in part with people coming in from Brittany and choosing to signal and memorialize their identity by building wedge-shaped megalithic tombs that harked back to ancient funerary traditions back home.

Below: **Pot from Kilmartin, Scotland, combining features from Irish and Yorkshire Food Vessel design.**

Opposite page: **Miniature macehead pendants found at Tara show the adoption of Orkney designs.**

EARLY BRONZE AGE INTERACTIONS

Moving forward again, to the Early Bronze Age around 2200 BC, by now copper from Ross Island would have circulated around Ireland, and been exported to Britain and perhaps also Brittany, for several generations. Interactions with Britain were massively boosted when continental prospectors discovered tin (and also gold) in Cornwall around 2200 BC. Both metals were exported to south-west Ireland where the tin was alloyed with copper to make bronze and the gold was made into lunulae and other objects.

The pattern of the flow of Irish metal makes it clear that those people who were able to control its movement 'got rich quick', as Stuart Needham has outlined (Needham 2004). This is certainly the case with Kilmartin Glen in the west of Scotland near the southern end of the Great Glen – the main route up to a major metalworking centre in north-east Scotland. The entrepreneurial elite in Kilmartin who got their metal supplies from Ireland built a series of ostentatious funerary mounds along the bottom of Kilmartin Glen. In one of these, they carved images of the source of their wealth – that is, the flat metal axeheads that they were trading – on to a pre-existing slab of rock bearing ancient Atlantic rock art motifs and they used it as the capstone of their cist.

They also obtained fine Irish-style pots and even got a potter to make a curious hybrid *(left)*. The top part is a classic Irish Bowl Food Vessel but the four stumpy little feet are characteristic of Food Vessels in

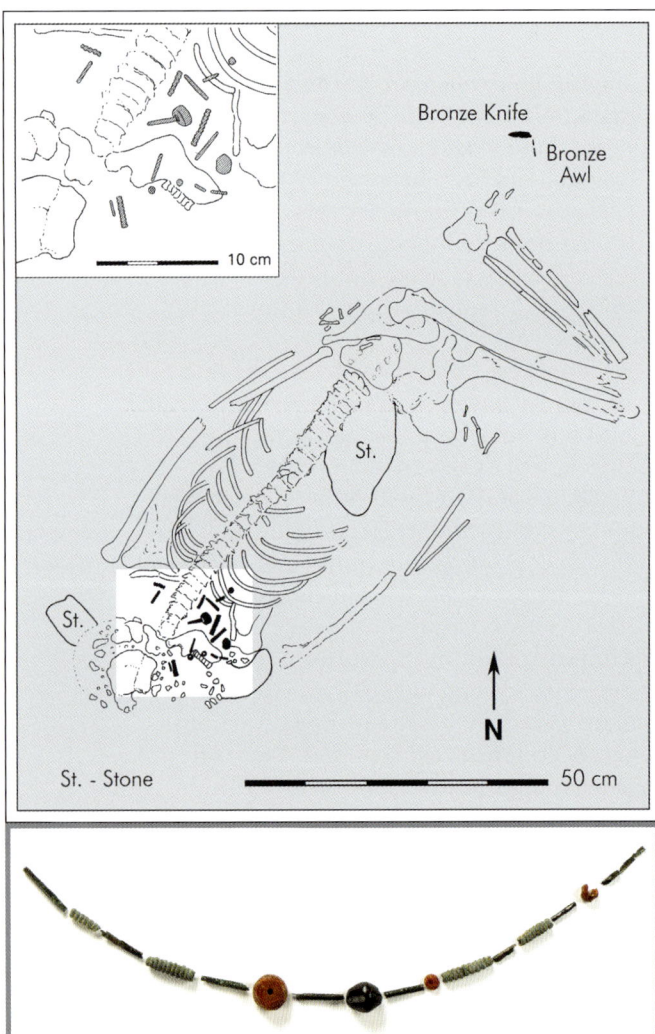

Top: **The young man who was buried at the Mound of the Hostages, Tara.**

Above: **Necklace found with the young man.**

Yorkshire. Another sign of connections was the use of their wealth to acquire fine spacer-plate necklaces made of jet from around Whitby in North Yorkshire. Made in Yorkshire by specialist jet workers, and worn by high status women, these necklaces were skeuomorphs of Irish gold lunulae.

A final example of the phenomenon of long-distance elite travel for cosmological acquisition, this time dating to around 1750 BC, concerns the fascinating individual who is buried in the mound of the Neolithic passage tomb called The Mound of the Hostages at Tara. This by-then ancient monument would have been a very special and exclusive place of burial, and this person's grave is unusual in several respects, including the fact that the deceased was buried, rather than cremated (as other Early Bronze Age individuals had been), and that it is the latest grave on the mound.

Excavated in the 1950s and osteologically identified as a young man, the occupant of this grave, dubbed 'Tara Boy', was buried with female trappings – a composite necklace made from faience, bronze, amber and jet, a bronze awl and a little knife or razor, much more slender than razors used by males at that time. Isotopic analysis revealed that this individual had not been raised in the Tara area but probably somewhere else in Ireland. The composite necklace, with its variety of precious materials, may well have been credited with special powers and worn as an amulet, thereby making this a kind of supernatural 'power dressing'. It is a type of high-status female artefact that was particularly popular in and around the Stonehenge area in southern England while, in contrast, such necklaces are very rare in Ireland. It may be that 'Tara Boy' had travelled over to Wessex to witness the solstitial ceremonies at Stonehenge and acquired the necklace there, later adding further beads back in Ireland. Stonehenge had long attracted visitors from far and wide, just as Orkney and Brú na Bóinne had done in previous centuries. From 2000 BC onwards, when new sources of copper were being mined in Ireland and Britain and when the tin supply system was reorganized, the area around Stonehenge seems to have become a centre for the ostentatious display of wealth and power, especially in the burial of the dead. Perhaps the necklace had been a diplomatic gift from a member of the Wessex elite to a visiting member of the elite who controlled the area around Tara.

There remain many questions about this person, not least that of biological sex, which is being investigated further. For now, 'Tara Boy' remains a person of mystery who reminds us once again of the capacity that certain members of society had to undertake long-distance journeys and to engage with the wider world outside of Ireland.

Acknowledgements

I want to thank Una MacConville and Sharon Greene for giving me the very great honour and privilege of participating in such a fabulous and stimulating conference in honour of George Eogan. And thanks, too, to all of my wonderful Irish friends and colleagues, including Ken Williams, who generously allowed me to reproduce their images in my lecture and in this paper.

BIBLIOGRAPHY

Bradley, R.J. 2022. *A comparative study of rock art in later prehistoric Europe*. Cambridge: Cambridge University Press.

Cassen, S., Pétrequin, P., Boujot, C., Dominguez-Bella, S., Guiavarc'h, M. and Querré, G. 2010. Measuring distinction in the megalithic architecture of the Carnac region: from sign to material. *Journal of Neolithic Archaeology* [Online]. 12 (2), pp1–49. Available from: https://doi.org/10.12766/jna.2010.45. [Accessed 16 June 2023].

Cassidy, L.M., Ó Maoldúin, R., Kador, T., Lynch, A., Jones, C., the late Woodman, P.C., Murphy, E.M., Ramsey, G., Dowd, M., Noonan, A., Campbell, C., Jones, E.R., Mattiangeli, V. and Bradley, D.G. 2020. A dynastic elite in monumental Neolithic society. *Nature* [Online]. 582, pp384–8. Available from: https://doi.org/10.1038/s41586-020-2378-6 (Accessed 16 June 2023].

Eogan, G. 1980. Objects with Iberian affinities from Knowth, Ireland. *Revista de Guimãraes* 89, pp3–7.

Helms, M. W. 1988. *Ulysses' sail: an ethnographic odyssey of power, knowledge, and geographical distance*. Princeton: Princeton University Press.

Lynch, A. 2014. *Poulnabrone: An Early Neolithic Portal Tomb in Ireland*. Department of Arts, Heritage and the Gaeltacht, Archaeological Monograph Series, 9. Dublin: The Stationery Office.

Needham, S.P. 2004. Migdale-Marnoch: sunburst of Scottish metallurgy *IN*: Shepherd, I.A.G. and Barclay, G.J. (eds.) *Scotland in Ancient Europe: the Neolithic and Early Bronze Age of Scotland in their European context*. Edinburgh: Society of Antiquaries of Scotland. pp217–245.

Sheehy Skeffington, M. and Scott, N. 2022. The strawberry tree in Ireland. *Archaeology Ireland* 36 (2), pp24–9.

Valdez-Tullett, J. 2019. *Design and connectivity: the case of Atlantic rock art*. International Series 2932. Archaeology of Prehistoric Rock Art. Volume 1. Oxford: BAR Publishing.

Chapter 7:

I was lucky enough as a very young curator to meet Professor Eogan for the first time on the Bronze Age Study Group and he immediately put me at ease by asking if he could come to the British Museum to study our lockring collection. He had published that many years previously so it was a typically kind gesture to put a young curator at ease.

DR NEIL WILKIN

Lives that Bind: Three Stories from the World of Stonehenge

Dr Neil Wilkin is curator of Early Europe at the British Museum. He was lead curator of the World of Stonehenge exhibition at the museum in 2022. The exhibition reflected his passion to use certain artefacts to introduce a wider audience to prehistory and to help them engage with the lives of people who lived then. In this paper, he uses the stories of three important recent discoveries from the world of Stonehenge to show the links between prehistoric communities in Yorkshire, Stonehenge, Orkney and Ireland.

The World of Stonehenge exhibition held in London in 2022 attracted over 190,000 visitors and over a million people tuned in to online events, talks and tours of the exhibition, which shows the value and power of prehistory to a much wider audience than just archaeologists and people who are passionate or interested in this subject.

With over 1,000 objects from 36 different lenders, there was much for audiences to choose from. However, one of the most remarkable objects in the exhibition was the carved flint macehead found at the eastern tomb at Knowth, placed at the beginning of the exhibition, welcoming visitors in with its stony face. We were able to put it together with three other maceheads of the Maesmor type from the Irish Sea zone. I think the public response shows the power of this object, particularly the Knowth object but also those other Maesmor maceheads, the way in which they appeal and attract through time and across subject specialisms as well.

The exhibition used Stonehenge as a gateway. For the majority of the public in England and across Britain, Stonehenge is one of the few touchstones they have to this period of deep history and for that reason it provides a powerful portal to the period.

In delivering the exhibition, we wanted to bring the idea that there is not just one Stonehenge, there are many different, but equally important, monuments dotted across both Britain and Ireland but also, importantly, across the whole of north-west Europe. Stonehenge changed dramatically through time. Also, it is a monument that tells us about people, it is not an abstract, dry, curated object in a field, it is about communities coming together, as seen every summer and winter solstice. The exhibition was about putting the people back into the narrative

Opposite page: **The World of Stonehenge exhibition at the British Museum in 2022.**

through objects. That was really what we were trying to do. The obvious but really important point is that we can only understand why anyone would be motivated and passionate enough to build monuments like Stonehenge if we understand the worlds in which they were situated, understand what the people were like, what motivated the communities (Barrett and Boyd 2019). So, that need for a bigger picture and for a human story was at the heart of what we were trying to achieve.

WEAVING STORIES

When we talk about this time period, we need to find a way, particularly when we are talking to the widest possible audience, of weaving together the stories of the monuments in the landscapes with the stories of people like you and I, because there is still a barrier. When we go back beyond written texts, to a time before that, there is still something of an assumption that these people were not 'like us', that they did not live emotional, personal lives, when I think we all know that they did. The stories are only coming into focus more now thanks to new discoveries that are being made every year, every day, but also thanks to the new scientific techniques

Above: **Maesmor-type maceheads from Ireland, Scotland and Wales on display at the World of Stonehenge exhibition.**

Opposite page: **Stonehenge: ceremonial landscapes are found across the whole of north-west Europe.**

and ways of studying material culture and monuments. It is an exciting time to be thinking about some of these questions and the integration of the different scales of study that we can pursue.

The first story takes us to Stonehenge of 3000 BC, when the blue stones are brought from Wales over 290 kilometres to Salisbury Plain. This was an astonishing achievement of will-power. This is not just some abstract distance coverage; this is people, communities, actively being employed and taking time out of what must have been busy, sometimes dangerous, lives to move these stones from Wales to this new location on Salisbury Plain and to build this new monument, to

undertake this act of love in some ways. It did not stand in isolation, it connected with what was happening right across Britain, Ireland and Europe in terms of the formation of these monuments and in particular in Britain, of course, the idea of the henge monument coming into focus.

This was a moment of connectivity. The material culture of 3000 BC, the Late Neolithic, linked up different regions of Britain and Ireland. Through Grooved Ware pottery, portable objects like the Maesmor maceheads and many other types of objects, we see increased connectivity around this time.

OBJECTS AND EMOTION

The object at the heart of the first story is a new discovery that was made, or at least made public, just before the Stonehenge exhibition opened, at a site called Burton Agnes on the Yorkshire Wolds, excavated by Allen Archaeol-

Above: **Drum-shaped chalk cylinder, ball and pin found with a burial at Burton Agnes, Yorkshire.**

Opposite page: **Decoration on three chalk drums found at a single child's burial in Folkton, Yorkshire, two of which bear a 'face' motif.**

ogy Ltd. I consider it to be one of the most important Neolithic objects discovered in England in the last 100–150 years. Found in a grave group burial with three children, and those children were all different ages, it is a chalk cylinder, sometimes called a 'drum' but is not a musical instrument, it is called that just to describe the shape, the form. It was found with a small chalk ball and a bone pin.

The beautifully carved chalk ball I found to be one of the most emotional objects in the whole exhibition because you could imagine it held in a small child's hand. It collapsed time. That is what objects can do, they can collapse time, they can bring us back to that moment in 3000 BC when a child has passed away and bring back the emotion of that moment.

There was also a very interesting bone pin that is still being studied for species. It is not so dissimilar to pins from other sites including Stonehenge, of course, and sites like the burial mound at Duggleby Howe in East Yorkshire and the recently excavated monument complex at Forteviot in the east of Scotland. The chalk ball is paralleled well by finds at other important Late Neolithic sites, including Bulford near Stonehenge, a recent excavation (Wessex Archaeology n.d.), and also sites like Grime's Graves, where these

ball and pin to the period from around 3000 BC to about a century afterwards, at the start of the Grooved Ware phenomenon.

What made this new discovery and new dating evidence so important is that it was not the first time we had seen one of these objects. In fact, we had seen three. These were from the famous site of Folkton, just off the Yorkshire Wolds, about half a day's walk, about 13 miles north of where the new discovery was made at Burton Agnes. At Folkton, three chalk cylinders of a very similar type were buried with one child and, in the new discovery, one chalk cylinder was found with three children. So, in both cases, we have four 'entities', if we want to call them that; one child and three cylinders and then, in the new

objects have been interpreted as being fertility symbols (Teather 2016). A radiocarbon date obtained from the bone of one of the three children allows us to date the chalk cylinder,

Above and below: **(Figs 6a & 6b) Separate areas of decoration on the Burton Agnes drum.**

Opposite page: **A comparison of the bands of decoration found on the Burton Agnes drum (bottom) and the three Folkton drums.**

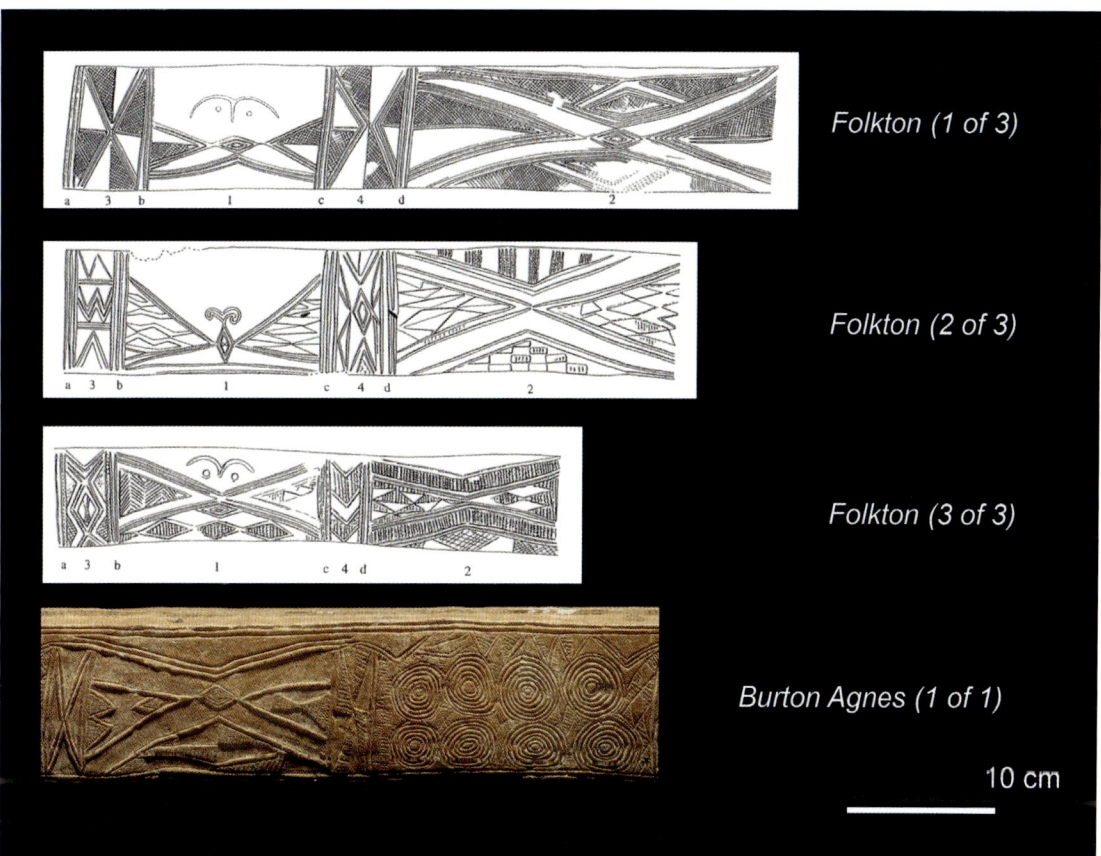

Folkton (1 of 3)

Folkton (2 of 3)

Folkton (3 of 3)

Burton Agnes (1 of 1)

10 cm

discovery, three children and one cylinder. So already there is a strong sense of structure and symbolism to these burials.

Decorative Motifs

The decoration of the Folkton drums has been studied many times, particularly by Ian Longworth (Longworth 1999) of the British Museum, who observed that the decorative motifs were very similar to Grooved Ware pottery, from the very end of Grooved Ware, close to the Beaker period, he thought. We know now from the radiocarbon date obtained from the Burton Agnes burial that they are in fact from about 400–500 years earlier. Longworth also observed that there were parallels for the decoration in the wider repertoire of rock art and passage grave art, although this point is subject to a lot of caveats. It is not as easy as saying that the motifs on these drums directly connect to sites like Knowth and Newgrange but they are part of that much wider Late Neolithic, Grooved Ware, artistic repertoire and that is what makes them so intriguing and beguiling.

On to the new Burton Agnes drum. It has several new elements that have not been seen before and that were not on the Folkton drums (Varndell and Wilkin 2022). One such element is that three holes have been drilled in the top of the chalk cylinder. It is very interesting that there should be three, making one wonder if there is one hole for each of the children that were buried with the drum. Another interesting detail is that the decoration made in between the three holes at the top is relatively complete, although not perhaps finished, line and false relief. Then, in the second band there is line decoration only. In the third band, there is a completely undecorated surface. This might indicate that the object was never finished, that there was haste before it was buried with the three children. Another possibility is that this was quite an intentional decision, perhaps showing three different periods of life, of completeness, which would represent the fact that in the grave there were children of three different ages, and the grading, as it were, of the decoration was intended to reference the grading of the children within the grave.

Another point of interest about the structure of the decoration is that it can be viewed as having four separate blocks, or units, of decoration. Ian Longworth was able to identify this when he studied the Folkton drums for his 1999 paper (ibid.). On the new, Burton Agnes drum there is a similar structure, with two (longer) landscape-orientated panels and two (shorter) portrait-orientated panels.

Similarities and differences between the decoration of the four drums raise the issue of to what extent we should see them as products of the same logic or embodiment of the same structural principles.

There are also some very interesting motifs on the Folkton drums that do not (or very rarely) occur in other types of pottery or rock art, which are the face motifs. Their presence may support the idea that the drums had

---

Below: **The alignment of Stonehenge and the installation of the sarsen stones** *(opposite page)* **occurred around 2500 BC.**

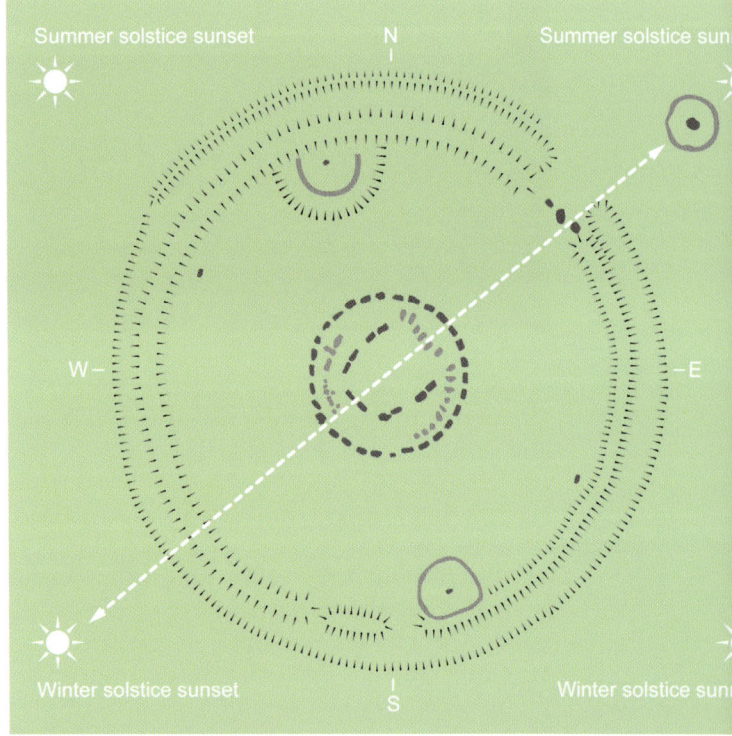

some kind of equivalence with the small bodies they were buried with. Could they represent idols or even gods? There is a face motif on two of the Folkton drums. Face motifs from around the same time are known from other parts of Europe. So, on Zealand in Denmark, there are about 100 face pots that date to around 3000 to 2900 BC – the period to which we know now the drums probably belong. These are funerary objects, often buried in passage tombs, which gives an interesting parallel. There is also a much wider context for face motifs as they are found across Iberia, which has been studied by Chris Scarre (2017). So, these faces are found right across Europe at this time.

SOLAR MOTIF

There appears to be a solar motif on the top of the new Burton Agnes drum – the cross-inside-a-circle motif. As Stuart Needham (pers. comm.) has pointed out, the largest of the Folkton drums has at the top a similar motif in the form of a four-pointed star. Again from Denmark and also from the Funnel Beaker culture, it is interesting that there are solar symbols on discs dating from around the same time as the Burton Agnes and Folkton drums, producing the possibility of continental connections between Yorkshire and the near Continent.

Closer to home, several solar symbols are found on Grooved Ware pots, including ones from Links of Noltland on Orkney (Sheridan 1999). Also, from Flagstones in Dorchester, there is a very interesting little cup, which is similar to one from Stonehenge. In the centre of the little cup there is one of the cross-inside-a-circle motifs. It is fascinating to think that 500 years before the introduction of metal, which we tend to associate with these types of symbols, including several referred to by Mary Cahill in her paper about the gold disc introduced by Beaker people (Cahill 2015), this symbol already may have had currency.

A further point to be made about the

context of these objects is that they were graded when they were put in the grave. So, the smallest of the chalk drums was placed at the top of the grave near the head and the largest drum was near the waist. That is exactly what is found in the new Burton Agnes burial, except that it is not the drums that are graded, it is actually the children in the grave that are graded with, first, the eldest child between 10 and 12 years, then the intermediary child, 6 to 9 years, and then the youngest child aged 3 to 5 years in that order.

To make the final point about this burial, the solar motif on the top of the drum is positioned at the east end of the grave where the children were, perhaps associated with the rising sun, perhaps connecting the children's deaths with the cosmos and return of the sun.

The second story that I will discuss takes place during a period when Stonehenge was being transformed into the monument that you and I would recognize today, when the sarsen monument went up and the monument was aligned on the midwinter and midsummer sun or, at least, that alignment was really enshrined at this time. It is around this time that we see the arrival of the Beaker people and it is interesting to consider how the building boom of which Stonehenge is one example interacted with the new introduction of the Beaker people in the twenty-fifth century BC. There is much to be said still about the relationships between the Grooved Ware and the Beaker cultures and beliefs but what we have seen from the Burton Agnes drum is the possibility that there was a real meeting of minds between the two on several key aspects of cosmology and there was not necessarily a total break in

symbolic language or cosmology between these peoples.

Heirloom Objects

Returning to the British Museum exhibition, we wanted to tell the story of ancient people not just through the showiest objects we could display but through some of the more

Opposite page: **Artist's impression of how the woman buried at Horton might have looked, with her gold beads** *(above)* **and the type of gold basket ornaments from which her beads could have been recycled** *(below)*.

personal stories that we could talk about. In a relatively new discovery made by Wessex Archaeology (Needham and Sheridan 2014), at a site called Horton, near Windsor, which has not yet been fully published, a woman was buried – and for us it was very important that we had female graves, a female figure, in the exhibition and not just the male-dominant elite figures that we tend to read about in older prehistories – and she was buried with amber buttons, with a beautiful little necklace of lignite disc beads but also with some unassuming but important gold beads that Stuart Needham has studied (Needham n.d.). He made a very interesting observation that those gold beads could have been reworked or reused from an older object that could have been, perhaps, like one of the basket ornaments *(below left)* that are among some of the earliest primary gold. So, there is the possibility of the curation and passing down of heirlooms and objects that were then being transformed into new objects, in almost a material parallel – or alternative – for genetic connections (See Brück, p 63).

One of the stars of the exhibition was the Amesbury Archer. We have known for over a decade that the Archer was an immigrant to England who came probably from the foothills of the Alps and was buried close to Stonehenge with great ceremony. This individual has been held up as a kind of exemplar for the new Beaker people. However, another man was buried nearby (the so-called Archer's Companion) who had the basket ornaments of the type seen at bottom left but without any of the sort of riches that the Amesbury Archer was buried with. The fact that both men shared a rare bone struc-

ture in their feet has been taken as evidence that they were closely related. Recent aDNA analysis has, however, suggested they were not as closely related as once thought

Above: **Artefacts found buried with the Amesbury Archer close to Stonehenge.**

Opposite page: **The Shropshire sun pendant, which was thrown into a bog around 1000–800 BC.**

(Fitzpatrick *et al.* 2022). In fact, the genetics suggest that they were quite far removed and even may have been third-generation relatives, which would be great-grandfather to great-grandson.

Using that knowledge, to go back to the woman who was buried at Horton, we may have a glimpse of the considerable generational time, perhaps even about 80 years, over which objects had been passed and curated, which puts the kind of objects that

we study into a new light. It brings us into a new era, one not so much prehistory as a kind of protohistory. There is a very important caveat, however, and that is that David Reich and his fellow geneticists (ibid.) could not rule out that there was in fact no genetic relationship between the Companion and the Archer. It is a really important salient reminder that we cannot always assume that the only important relationships are genetic. We are going to find individuals that are not genetically related but who are importantly,

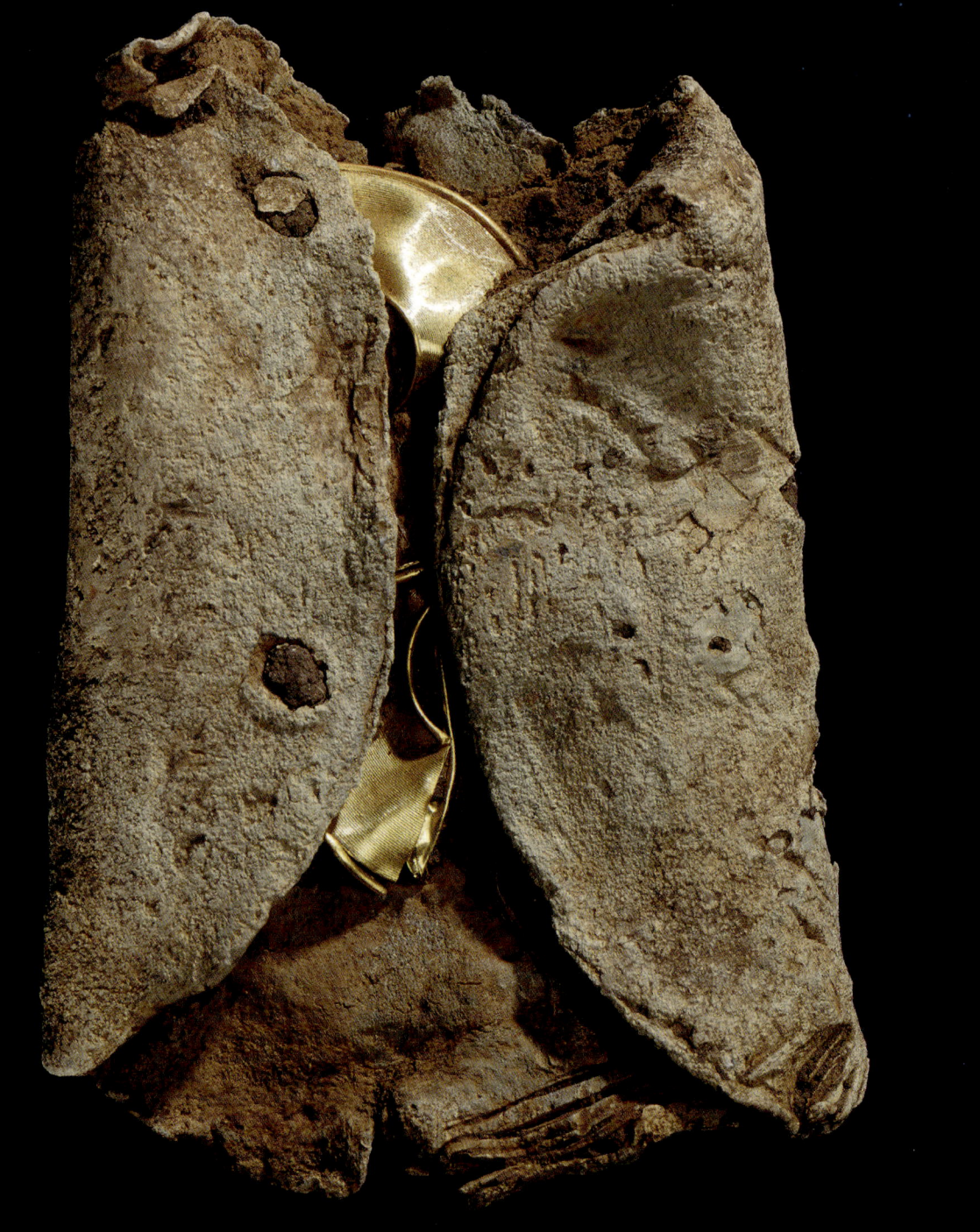

socially and culturally related, so we still need the objects and the object studies to put things into fuller context.

Sacrificial Offerings

In the final part of the British Museum exhibition we wanted to tell the story of how Stonehenge lost its power, how it lost its charm if you like. A big part of that is the story of trade and exchange along the south coast of England and of the way that the power dynamic shifted away from inland Wessex towards the south and south-east coasts of England from around 1500 BC and how other interests, from barrows to field systems (Needham pp74–87), became the dominant expressions of society, kinship and power. We start at this time to see burial becoming less important and the deposition – or sacrifice – of valuables, particularly gold-work, becoming more and more important.

A new object discovered a few years before the Stonehenge exhibition, called the Shropshire sun pendant, was thrown into a bog in Shropshire around 1000 or perhaps closer to 800 BC. It is an astonishing object, very beautifully engraved and reversible, possibly showing a rising or setting sun. It is constructed in a really exquisite way from just two sheets of gold. The very skilled gold-worker, Brian Clarke, who worked on making a replica of the pendant, suggested that pro-

bably it was kept together by internal solder, which is as difficult as it sounds.

There are some intriguing connections between the pendant and objects from Ireland. In the exhibition, we were very lucky to be able to display it side by side with the Bog of Allen bulla, from the National Museum of Ireland, and to draw parallels between them. It is not exactly the same shape but it does have some very interesting similarities both in decoration and form. It should be said that the Bog of Allen bulla has a lead core. That is significant because of another discovery made close to the find spot of the pendant: a sheet of lead used to wrap two gold lock-rings whose metal composition is very similar to the Shropshire pendant, thus helping with its dating and unravelling its wider cultural and technological context.

The figure on page 156 gives a sense of what one of those lock-rings would have looked like at the time that it was new and uncrumpled. Some of the technology of their construction, particularly the very fine tubing around the outside of the lock-ring, is paralleled in the way that the pendant has been constructed (Eogan 1969). So, there are some nice connections. After the pendant was found we excavated the find spot to identify what the landscape had been like at this time. We were able to discern that it had been a flooded landscape with pools of water. Into the pool of water, this object was thrown intentionally and the lead parcel that wrapped up those lock-rings, sealing them in, was also thrown into this watery landscape.

This was a moment of real change and transformation in the sense that, at this time, people were sacrificing a huge amount of

Opposite page: **Two gold lock-rings enclosed in a lead sheet, which also were deposited close to the sun pendant. Their metal composition is very similar to that of the pendant.**

wealth into rivers, into bogs. It is interesting to speculate and think about why that might have been. One of the senses that we get is that society was under pressure for social and perhaps environmental reasons and that some of these offerings might have been a way of speaking to those pressures, trying to stop those pressures. Today perhaps, we can all identify with that, with these pressures. They are very much of the moment.

The pendant summed up what we were trying to achieve with the exhibition and that was to express the importance of creativity at this time. These were incredibly skilled people and we hope we showed that to a wide public audience. It also showed connectivity. The pendant sums up the distinct connections between places like England but also Ireland and the Continent. Finally, there is the enduring and critical importance of solar symbolism, of the sun filling the chamber at Knowth but also then transformed into the decoration on lunulae, then transformed thousands of years later into an object like the pendant, which was thrown then into a bog, which marks the end of the Bronze Age, the end of a cycle and the beginning of a new era associated with iron and with the development of a new style of 'Celtic' art – a very different story altogether.

To conclude by quoting the archaeologist Jacquetta Hawkes (1910–96), 'Every age has the Stonehenge it deserves – or desires'. What we tried to show in the Stonehenge

---

Above left: **Gold tubing on lock-rings, including this example from Gaerwen, Wales, have parallels with the construction of the sun pendant** *(left)*.

exhibition and what I hope I have glimpsed here is that, actually, what is really important for sites like Stonehenge and Knowth and Newgrange is that we remind ourselves of their human stories and the wider set of connections that they always existed within.

Acknowledgements

I am extremely grateful for the invitation to speak at the Boyne and Beyond conference in celebration of Professor Eogan's legacy and to all at *Archaeology Ireland* and Wordwell Ltd for their assistance and patience, especially Peigín Doyle and Una MacConville. Thanks are also due to Mark Allen, Jill Cook, Duncan Garrow, Stuart Needham, Alison Sheridan, Gillian Varndell, Craig Williams and Jennifer Wexler for their help in preparing this contribution although all errors remain my own. The World of Stonehenge exhibition would not have been at all possible without the generosity of many lenders including The National Museum of Wales, The National Museums Scotland but particularly The National Museum of Ireland, who were one of our key lenders and lent us some remarkable objects.

BIBLIOGRAPHY

Barrett, J.C. and Boyd, M.J. 2019. *From Stonehenge to Mycenae: The Challenges of Archaeological Interpretation.* London: Bloomsbury.

Cahill, M. 2015. Here comes the sun. *Archaeology Ireland.* 29(1) Spring 2015, pp26–33.

Eogan, G., 1969. Lock-Rings of the Late Bronze Age. *Proceedings of the Royal Irish Academy.* (67C), pp93–148.

Fitzpatrick, A., McKinley, J., Barclay, A., Armit, I., Olalde, I. and Reich, D. 2022. Family ties: deciphering the DNA of the Amesbury Archer and the Companion. *Current Archaeology.* March 2022, pp50–53.

Longworth, I. 1999.The Folkton Drums Unpicked *IN*: Cleal, R. and MacSween, A. (eds.) *Grooved Ware in Britain and Ireland,* Neolithic Studies Group Seminar Papers 3, Oxford: Oxbow Books, pp83–88.

Teather, A. 2016. *Mining and Materiality: Neolithic Chalk Artefacts and their Depositional Contexts in Southern Britain.* Oxford: Archaeopress.

Needham, S. and Sheridan, J.A. 2014. Chalcolithic and Early Bronze Age goldwork from Britain: new finds and new perspectives *IN*: Meller, H., Pernicka, E. and Risch, R. (eds.) *Metals of Power: Early Gold and Silver. Proceedings of the 6th Archaeological Congress of Central Germany,* 2013. Halle: Landesmuseum für Vorgeschicht Halle, pp903–41.

Needham, S. n.d. Report on gold ornaments from Kingsmead Quarry, Horton. Unpublished report for Wessex Archaeology.

Scarre, C. 2017. Neolithic figurines of Western Europe *IN*: Insoll, T. (ed.) *The Oxford handbook of prehistoric figurines.* Oxford: Oxford University Press, pp877–900.

Sheridan, J.A. 1999. Grooved Ware from the Links of Noltland, Orkney *IN*: Cleal, R. and MacSween, A. (eds.) *Grooved Ware in Britain and Ireland,* Neolithic Studies Group Seminar Papers 3, Oxford: Oxbow Books, pp112–24.

Varndell, G. and Wilkin, N. 2022. Report on the grave group of chalk 'drum', chalk ball and bone pin from grave pit [7251], Burton Agnes, East Yorkshire, England. Unpublished report for Allen Archaeology Ltd.

Wessex Archaeology. n.d. Bulford. https://www.wessexarch.co.uk/our-work/bulford (accessed 26 May 2023).

IMAGE CREDITS

COVER:
  Knowth. © Photographic Archive, National Monuments Service, Government of Ireland.

FOREWORD:
Pages 4-7
  Newgrange. © Photographic Archive, National Monuments Service, Government of Ireland.
  Jamb stone at Knowth. Courtesy of Ken Williams.

INTRODUCTION:
Pages 8
  George Eogan excavating at Fourknocks in July 1952. Courtesy of James Eogan.

CHAPTER 1:
What Lies Beneath? Uncovering the story of Knowth through time

Page 11
  The excavations in the early 1970s, looking north-east, with the cuttings into the large mound visible centre. © Leo Swan.

Pages 12–13
  LiDAR image of Brú na Bóinne with sites marked. Courtesy Meath County Council and the Discovery Programme.
  Knowth as it appeared in 1963, a year after excavations started, looking to the south-west. Reproduced with permission of the Cambridge Collection of Aerial Photography (©) Copyright reserved.

Pages 14–15
  Aerial view Knowth today. Courtesy of Ken Williams.
  Artist's impression of settlement at Knowth in the Early Neolithic. Courtesy of Steve Doogan.

Pages 16–17
  Carinated Bowl pottery similar to this recon-structed vessel were found at Knowth. Courtesy of Graham Taylor.
  The location of Houses A and B in relation to the large mound. Image Kerri Cleary and Chiara Mazzanti, from G. Eogan and E. Shee Twohig 2022, *Excavations at Knowth 7 - The megalithic art of the passage tombs at Knowth*, County Meath. © RIA.

Pages 18–19
  Artist's impression of the building of the large mound with associated structures on the site. Courtesy of Steve Doogan.
  The footprint of the large tomb in its first and second stages, with the V-shaped entrances visible in the first phase. Elizabeth Shee Twohig and Robin Turk from Eogan and Shee Twohig 2022, *Excavations at Knowth 7*. © RIA.

Pages 20–21
  The splayed entrance to the east tomb uncovered during excavation. Courtesy of Eimear Meegan and Knowth Archive.
  Extended west passage that enlarged tomb 1C. Courtesy of Ken Williams.

Pages 23
  Looking into the north recess of the east tomb with the basin stone sitting behind two free-standing jamb stones at the entrance. Courtesy of Ken Williams.

Pages 24
  Artefacts from the eastern tomb included pendants and beads. Courtesy of Ken Williams.

Page 26-27
  Displaced corbel 5/6 and Orthostat 5 in the outer western passage of the large mound, behind which human bone was placed in the Late Neolithic. From Eogan and Kerri Cleary 2017, *Excavations at Knowth 6 - The passage tomb archaeology of the Great Mound at Knowth*. © RIA.
  The presence of Beaker pottery showed that Knowth remained an important site in the Chalcolithic period. Courtesy of Ken Williams.

Pages 28–29
  The burial placement of 'The Gamblers' with their accompanying gaming pieces, from the Late Iron Age. From Eogan et al. 2012, *Excavations at Knowth 5 - The archaeology of Knowth in the first and second millennia AD*. © RIA.
  Artist's impression of Knowth in the Early Medieval period when the mound was altered into a stepped shape with (left) a causeway to the top. Courtesy of Steve Doogan.

Pages 30–31
  The outer passages of the large mound were realigned to link with later souterrains. Courtesy of Ken Williams.

Pages 32–33
  The summit of the mound was levelled in the Late Medieval to support a stone wall and farm buildings. Courtesy of Steve Doogan.
  George Eogan and members of the excavation team working at the west tomb in 1967. © Photographic Archive, National Monuments Service, Government of Ireland.

CHAPTER 2:
Exploring the Life Cycle of a Forgotten Monument: the Dowth Hall Passage Tomb Excavation

Pages 36–37

    The surviving interior of tomb 1 of Dowth Hall passage tomb. Courtesy of Ken Williams.

Pages 38–39

    Map of the UNESCO World Heritage Site of the Bend of the Boyne, showing location of Dowth Hall estate. The core area is shown in pink and the estate in lilac. Original Image produced by Stephen Davis on OSI base map.

    One of the earliest images of Dowth Hall, a photograph of the drawing room from 1915. *Georgian Mansions in Ireland: With Some Account of the Evolution of Georgian Architecture and Decoration.* Plate XLVII. Dublin: Dublin University Press.

Pages 40–41

    Aerial photograph (© OSI) of Dowth Hall and its environs, showing Dowth Henge, the passage tombs at Sites I and J, and Dowth passage tomb. Original Image produced by Stephen Davis on OSI base map.

    Dowth passage tomb in 1775, painted by the Dutch artist Gabriel Beranger. Reproduced with permission © RIA.

Pages 42–43

    Aerial photo of the Dowth Hall passage tomb showing burial chambers (Tombs 1 and 2), the kerb and the souterrain entrance. From Dowth Hall excavation archive. Courtesy of Ken Williams.

    The nine phases of activity at Dowth Hall passage tomb. Courtesy of Dave Hall.

Pages 44–45

    Aerial view of pits (outlined in white) that were sealed by the buried grass sod layers underneath the cairn. From Dowth Hall excavation archive. Courtesy of Ken Williams.

    Buried grass sod layers to the east of Tomb 1, with imprint of cairn stones still visible. From Dowth Hall excavation archive. Courtesy of Ken Williams.

    Aerial view of Tomb 1 showing stalls A, B and C, collapsed structural stones (T1.8-T1.12), and possible stone setting. From Dowth Hall excavation archive. Courtesy of Ken Williams.

Pages 46–47

    Stacked chevron motif on T1.9. Image Dowth Hall excavation archive.

    Stone concretions deposited on the floor of Stall A (Tomb 1). Image Dowth Hall excavation archive.

    Stone floor in Stall B that sealed a bone-rich layer. Composite photo showing collapsed orthostat in original upright position. Image Dowth Hall excavation archive.

Pages 48–49

    Aerial photograph of Tomb 2, showing side chamber (red) and ramp (white) with orthostats highlighted in colour and the modern tunnel wall on the top right. From Dowth Hall excavation archive. Courtesy of Ken Williams.

    Horizontal orthostat (T2.9) resting on vertical stone/prop within Tomb 2 side chamber. Dowth Hall excavation archive.

Pages 50–51

    Aerial view of five kerbstones. Dowth Hall excavation archive. Courtesy of Ken Williams.

    Decorated kerbstone (K2). Dowth Hall excavation archive. Courtesy of Ken Williams.

Pages 52–53

    View from original ground level, showing kerbstones, surviving cairn material (outlined in white), basement structures, including bowed projection, and southern elevation of Dowth Hall. Images Dowth Hall excavation archive.

    Post-excavation plan showing cairn, kerbstones and ditch that cut through the cairn slippage. Images Dowth Hall excavation archive.

Pages 54–55

    Entrance to souterrain (discovered in 2018). Dowth Hall excavation archive. Courtesy of Ken Williams.

    Souterrain interior viewed from chamber breach point. Roof stone (reused orthostat) visible in upper part of photograph. Dowth Hall excavation archive. Courtesy of Ken Williams.

Page 56

    Excavation of stone infill of Tomb 1, revealing collapsed structural stones ('deliberate decommissioning'). Dowth Hall excavation archive

CHAPTER 3:
Bronze Age Relations: Genetics, Kinship and Gender in Later Prehistory

Page 58

    Traditional interpretations of the Bronze Age saw male warriors and elites as central figures in society, a view that has a long pedigree, as this late nineteenth-century print demonstrates. Image from The New York Public Library https://digitalcollections.nypl.org.

Pages 60–61
Reconstruction of the excavated Bronze Age landscape at South Hornchurch, Greater London. Artist Roger Massey. Courtesy of © Essex County Council.

Sauk family. Studio portraits like these evocatively demonstrate how Indigenous families were expected to conform to Eurocentric norms. Photographed by F. A. Rinehart, Omaha, USA, 1899, image courtesy of © US Library of Congress.

Indian residential school, Fort Resolution, Northwest Territories. European colonial views on family and morality were imposed on Indigenous peoples leading in places to the removal of children from their families into institutions. Courtesy of Canada © Library and Archives Canada.

Page 62
In other cultural contexts, the boundary between people and animals is fluid and porous. Image courtesy of © Wellcome Collection.

Pages 64–65
Genetic relatives in the Stonehenge region. Circles represent females and triangles represent males. Image after fig. 5, Booth *et al.* 2021.

The Boscombe Bowmen, Wiltshire. Courtesy of © Wessex Archaeology.

Page 66
Young man and woman from the same matrilineage buried together at Trumpington Meadows. Courtesy of © Cambridge Archaeological Unit.

Pages 68–69
Ring ditch surrounding the graves of a number of women and children at Porton Down. The central grave had been accessed to manipulate the bones of a woman who may have been a person of significance. Courtesy of Andrews and Thomson, © Wessex Archaeology.

The recut grave at Over, Cambridgeshire. Top: primary burial; bottom: later burial inserted into the same grave. Burials of genetically-unrelated individuals challenge us to imagine other forms of kinship. Courtesy of © Cambridge Archaeological Unit.

Pages 70
Objects were often deposited at significant places, suggesting social and emotional links with landscape. The Dewerstone. Devon. Courtesy of Nilfanion.

Middle Bronze Age pot found in a cleft in the rock at the Dewerstone, Devon. Photograph by the author, with permission from Plymouth City Museum and Art Gallery.

Page 72
At Cliffs End Farm, a young woman was buried with her head resting on a cattle skull. Courtesy of McKinley *et al.*, 2014, © Wessex Archaeology.

CHAPTER 4:
From Barrowscape to Fieldscape: The first fields in the Rother Region of the Western Weald

Pages 74–75
The Rother Region within the wider landscape of south-east England. Courtesy of Sabine Stevenson; contains OS data © Crown copyright and database rights 2021 © Digimap Licence 656865). [volume fig 1.1 modified].

Barrows in the Rother Region; Petersfield Heath is located where the Rother changes course (arrowed). Courtesy of Sabine Stevenson; contains OS data © Crown copyright and database rights 2021 (100025252; Digimap Licence 656865).

Pages 76–77
Variations in barrow density in the Rother Region. Map courtesy of author. [volume fig 22.6 modified].

Territories of Early Bronze Age communities suggested for the Rother Region on the basis of barrows and contemporary evidence. Courtesy of Sabine Stevenson; contains OS data © Crown copyright and database rights 2021 (100025252; Digimap Licence 656865). [volume fig 21.3 modified].

Strontium isotope analysis of people buried at Petersfield Heath suggests diverse backgrounds. On right, burial site of a possible female who had moved during her lifetime. Courtesy of Stuart Needham; data from Schulting *et al.* (2021). [volume fig 11.10 modified].

Pages 78–79
Simplified time curves for round barrows, field systems, charred hazelnuts and charred cereals. Image courtesy of author; plant data based on Stevens & Fuller (2012).

The midwinter sun sets in the 'A3 notch' in the chalk ridge as viewed from Petersfield Heath. Courtesy of Sabine Stevenson.

The direction of midwinter sunset from the Petersfield Heath cemetery *c.*2000 BC (correction < 1˚). Barrows picked out in red are those with estimated volumes greater than 400m^3. [volume fig 22.11 modified]. Courtesy of Stuart Needham.

Pages 80–81
At The Devil's Jumps, Treyford Hill, the three largest barrows align on midwinter sunrise over the English Channel. Courtesy of Stuart Needham.

The 'solstice saltire' from Petersfield Heath cemetery. The alignments shown allow for the minor shifts since the Early Bronze Age and the inclination of observation lines. Courtesy of Stuart Needham and Sabine Stevenson; contains OS data © Crown copyright and database rights 2021 (100025252; Digimap Licence 656865). [volume fig 22.14].

Heath End, Duncton: interpretation of a ring ditch showing solstitial structure, excavated by Casper Johnson, Archaeology South-East. Courtesy of Stuart Needham.

Pages 82–83

Barrows and field systems on the South Downs between North Marden Down and Treyford Hill. Possible house platforms are also shown. Courtesy of Stuart Needham.

Core block of fields overlying the circumferential barrow group of Linchball Wood. The green-shaded strips are suggested to be the founder-fields and are aligned on midwinter sunrise and midsummer sunset. Courtesy of Stuart Needham.

Page 84

The core field blocks on North Marden Down (left) and Philliswood Down (right). The lighter grey tone is for fields suggested to have been next added. Courtesy of Stuart Needham.

Page 86

Goanah promontory, near Petworth, from the west showing some of the prominent lynchets. Courtesy of Stuart Needham.

CHAPTER 5:
Megalithic Art in the Boyne Valley and beyond

Pages 88–89

Newgrange and nearby passage tombs, looking east. Courtesy of Ken Williams.

Pages 90–91

Map of the Boyne Valley passage tombs and possible passage tombs, showing carved sites in red. Courtesy of Elizabeth Shee Twohig and Robin Turk in Eogan and Shee Twohig 2022.

Numbers of carved stones at Irish passage tombs and passage tomb-style stones. Courtesy of Elizabeth Shee Twohig and Robin Turk in Eogan and Shee Twohig 2022.

Pages 92–93

Cairn T interior, Loughcrew, County Meath, looking towards the backstone with sillstones in the foreground. Courtesy of Ken Williams.

Diagram showing the principal motifs of Standard Megalithic Art in Ireland. Image courtesy of Elizabeth Shee Twohig and Robin Turk in Eogan and Shee Twohig 2022.

Pages 94–95

The principal motifs in Standard Megalithic Art, recorded on Orthostat 8b, Tomb 14, Knowth. Image Eogan and Shee Twohig 2022.

Orthostat 81 in Tomb 1 West, Knowth, with Recycled Style Art. Courtesy of Ken Williams.

Pages 96–97

Orthostat L19 in the passage of Newgrange with Recycled Style Art and area picking. Courtesy of Ken Williams.

Orthostat C16 at Barclodiad y Gawres, Anglesey, Wales. Courtesy of Ken Williams.

Pages 98–99

Knowth Kerbstone 47, showing Large-scale Kerbstone Art style overlying an earlier spiral. Image Eogan and Shee Twohig 2022.

Newgrange Kerbstone 67. Courtesy of Ken Williams.

Page 100-101

Orthostat 69 Knowth Tomb 1 East, showing Ribbon-line art. Courtesy of Ken Williams.

Kerbstone 74, Knowth Tomb 1, at the entrance to the western tomb. Courtesy of Ken Williams.

Basin stone in Knowth Tomb 1 East. Courtesy of Ken Williams.

Pages 102–103

Dispersed picking in the inner section of Knowth Tomb 1 West. Courtesy of Ken Williams.

Amorphous Close-area Picking on corbels supporting the chamber capstone at Newgrange. Courtesy of Ken Williams.

Page 104

Amorphous Close-area Picking on corbels supporting the chamber capstone at Newgrange. Courtesy of Ken Williams.

Amorphous Close-area Picking on corbels and orthostats in the passage at Newgrange. Courtesy of Ken Williams.

A morphous Close-area Picking on RS16, the cross lintel supporting the corbelled roof at Newgrange. Courtesy of Ken Williams.

Pages 106–107

Maesmor type macehead from Knowth 1 East chamber, showing C-spiral motif. Image © National Museum of Ireland.

161

Carvings at Gavrinis passage tomb, Brittany. Courtesy of Ken Williams.

Page 108
Painting at Antelas passage tomb, Portugal. Courtesy of Ken Williams.

CHAPTER 6:
Ireland in the Wider Prehistoric World, 4300 – 1750 BC

Pages 110-111
Newgrange, Co Meath. Courtesy of Ken Williams.

Page 112
The carved stone 'idol' found outside the western passage of the main mound at Knowth, and similar to carvings from the Tagus estuary in Portugal. Drawing courtesy of Hilary Richardson. © RIA. Photograph courtesy of Ken Williams.

Pages 113-115
DNA evidence shows the spread of farming people to Ireland in the Early Neolithic, bringing a different way of life from that of the Mesolithic inhabitants. Ancestral diversity across European Neolithic populations before and after the spread of the Neolithization of Britain and Ireland. Images and captions courtesy Lara Cassidy.

The author's four-strand model of the spread of farming people in the Neolithic, three of which affected Ireland. Courtesy of Alison Sheridan.

Pages 116-117
Artist's impression of Ferriter's Cove Mesolithic landscape when the first Neolithic farming people arrived but failed to establish themselves. Woodman *et al*. 1999. From *Excavations at Ferriter's Cove 1983-95*. Artist Rhoda Cronin.

Closed megalithic chambers and simple passage tombs built by the second strand of immigrant farmers from Brittany around 4000 BC. **Carrowmore, Co Sligo**; courtesy of Andreas F. Borchert; **Carreg Samson**; courtesy of Llywelyn 2000 and **Achnacreebeag**, courtesy of V. Cummings, G. Ritchie, A. Sheridan.

Breton-style late Castellic pot found at the Achnacreebeag monument in western Scotland. Courtesy © National Museums Scotland.

Page 118
Jadeitite axes from the northern Alps, found at Rathmoghy (Kincraigy) Co. Donegal and Paslickstown, Co. Westmeath. Images © National Museum of Ireland.

Page 119
Artist's reconstruction of timber mortuary structure with facade from the Early Neolithic; this example is Street House, NE England. Drawing courtesy of © Blaise Vyner.

Pages 120-121
The distribution of Neolithic axeheads originating in the north Italian Alps. Courtesy of © *Projet JADE*.

Block of jadeitite and, beyond, the peak of Monte Viso in northern Italy, one of the two source areas of jadeitite axeheads. Courtesy of © *Projet JADE*.

Complete axe with head of Antrim porcellanite, found on the Isle of Lewis in the Outer Hebrides. Courtesy of © National Museums Scotland.

Pages 122-123
Hoard of Antrim flint items found at Auchenhoan, near Campbeltown, Scotland *(above)*, Arran pitchstone in north-east Ireland *(below left)*, and shared pottery designs *(below right)*, all evidence of close sea links. Image © National Museums Scotland.

Core of Arran pitchstone from Nappan, Co. Antrim. Courtesy of Alison Sheridan.

Shared pottery designs across the North Channel. Courtesy of Alison Sheridan.

Portal tombs in Ireland, Wales and Cornwall show early connections around the Irish Sea: Dyffryn Ardudwy portal tomb, Wales. Image courtesy of © Niall Sharples.

Page 124
Evolution of passage tombs in Co. Sligo from simple structures *(top, Carrowmore 7)* to increasingly aggrandized monuments *(centre, Listoghil, Carrowmore)*, culminating in Queen Maeve's Cairn on Knocknarea *(bottom)*. Photos by Jon Sullivan (PD Photo.org), Logopin and Jacknow, Wikimedia Commons.

Pages 126-127
'Guardian goddess' figures from Le Luffang, Brittany *(above)*. Image courtesy of Serge Cassen.

Knowth West *(right)*. Courtesy of Ken Williams.

Pages 128-129
Comparative plans of Knowth West (top) and Le Luffang with the positions of the 'Guardian goddess' stones indicated by stars. Courtesy of Alison Sheridan.

A similar style of high-relief megalithic art is found at tombs in Brú na Bóinne *(top)* and in the older passage tomb of Gavrinis, Morbihan, Brittany *(bottom)*. Photos: *(top)* © Photographic Archive, National Monuments Service, Government of Ireland; *(bottom)* By Ismoon (talk), Wikimedia Commons (replica of Gavrinis passage).

Page 130
The interior design of Newgrange passage tomb was replicated in the Orkney Islands at Maeshowe. Image © Almay.

Pages 132–133
The Stones of Stenness, a novel monument type in Orkney. By Calumsmith0308, Wikimedia Commons.

Carved stone objects from Orkney that were both symbolic objects of power and death-dealing weapons. Image © National Museums Scotland.

Pages 134–135
The southward spread of Grooved Ware (triangles) and of stone circles (squares) along Scotland's Atlantic facade. Courtesy of Alison Sheridan.

Bead found at Knowth is a miniature replica of a Scottish carved stone ball like the one found at the Ness of Brodgar. Courtesy of Ken Williams, © RIA.

Pages 136–137
Miniature macehead pendants found at Tara showed the adoption of Orkney designs. From *Tara: the Mound of the Hostages*. Muiris O'Sullivan, 2005, courtesy of Muiris O'Sullivan.

Pot from Kilmartin Glen, Scotland, combining features from Irish and Yorkshire Food Vessel designs. © Kilmartin Museum.

Page 138
The young man who was buried at the Mound of the Hostages, Tara. From *Tara: the Mound of the Hostages*. Muiris O'Sullivan, 2005, courtesy of Muiris O'Sullivan.

Necklace found with the young man. Image © National Museum of Ireland.

CHAPTER 7:
Lives that Bind: Three Stories from the World of Stonehenge

Page 140
The World of Stonehenge exhibition at the British Museum in 2022. Courtesy of Trustees of the British Museum.

Pages 142–143
Maesmor-type maceheads from Ireland, Scotland and Wales on display at the World of Stonehenge exhibition. Courtesy of Trustees of the British Museum.

Stonehenge: ceremonial landscapes are found across the whole of north-west Europe. Courtesy of English Heritage.

Pages 144–145
Drum-shaped chalk cylinder, ball and pin found with a burial at Burton Agnes, Yorkshire. Courtesy of Trustees of the British Museum.

Decoration on three chalk drums found at a single child's burial in Folkton, Yorkshire, two of which bear a 'face' motif. Courtesy of Trustees of the British Museum.

Pages 146–147
Separate areas of decoration on the Burton Agnes drum. Courtesy of Trustees of the British Museum.

A comparison of the bands of decoration found on the Burton Agnes drum (bottom) and the three Folkton drums. Courtesy of Ian Longworth and Trustees of the British Museum.

Pages 148–149
The alignment of Stonehenge. Courtesy of Trustees of the British Museum.

Image of the Sarsen Stones. Courtesy of Mike Pitts.

Pages 150–151
Artist's impression of how the woman buried at Horton might have looked, with her gold beads and the type of gold basket ornaments from which her beads could have been recycled. All imasge reproduced with permission © Wessex Archaeology.

Pages 152–153
Artefacts found buried with the Amesbury Archer close to Stonehenge. Image reproduced with permission © Wessex Archaeology.

The Shropshire sun pendant, which was thrown into a bog around 1000–800 BC. Courtesy of Trustees of the British Museum.

Page 154
Two gold lock-rings enclosed in a lead sheet, which also were deposited close to the sun pendant. Their metal composition is very similar to that of the pendant. Courtesy of Trustees of the British Museum.

Page 156
Gold tubing on lock-rings, including this example from Gaerwen, Wales, have parallels with the construction of the sun pendant. Courtesy of Trustees of the British Museum.

BIOGRAPHIES

DR KERRI CLEARY

was project coordinator and archaeological editor for *The passage tomb archaeology of the Great Mound at Knowth (Excavations at Knowth* vol. 6, RIA, 2017). She worked with Professor Eogan on the Knowth archive for over ten years and continues to research and publish on Irish archaeology, particularly the Neolithic and Bronze Age.

DR CLÍODHNA NÍ LIONÁIN

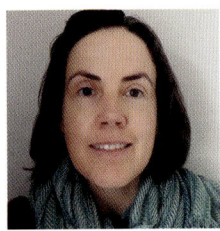

is the project archaeologist for the Devenish Lands at Dowth and an adjunct research fellow at UCD School of Archaeology. She is the site director for the excavation of the Dowth Hall passage tomb.

PROFESSOR JOANNA BRÜCK

is full professor in UCD School of Archaeology. Her recent books include *Personifying prehistory: relational ontologies in Bronze Age Britain and Ireland* (2019) and *The social context of technology: non-ferrous metalworking in later prehistoric Britain and Ireland* (2020).

DR STUART NEEDHAM

formerly curator of the European Bronze Age at the British Museum, is now an independent researcher.

DR ELIZABETH SHEE TWOHIG

former senior lecturer in the Department of Archaeology, University College Cork, has published extensively on megalithic art and megalithic tombs, most recently as archaeological editor of *The megalithic art of the passage tombs at Knowth, County Meath (Excavations at Knowth* vol. 7, RIA, 2022).

DR ALISON SHERIDAN

is emerita principal curator of Early Prehistory and currently a research associate with National Museums Scotland, Edinburgh, and a co-founder of the 'Boyne to Brodgar' research initiative. She has researched Irish prehistory for 45 years.

DR NEIL WILKIN

was lead curator of the 'World of Stonehenge' exhibition held at the British Museum (February–July 2022), where he has been a curator of Early Europe for ten years.

PEIGÍN DOYLE

is a writer and editor who has a lifelong curiosity about the history and heritage of place and how the world might have looked through our ancestors' eyes. She has written on many aspects of archaeology and heritage.